This book is dedicated to the citizens of New York City, who on September 11, 2001, saw the face of evil and responded with a faith, courage, and strength that makes me even more proud to be an American.

LOVE ME TO DEATH

Steve Jackson

PINNACLE BOOKS
Kensington Publishing Corp.
http://www.kensingtonbooks.com

Some names have been changed to protect the privacy of individuals connected to this story.

One

Suzanne Scott lay spread-eagled on the mattress, her wrists and ankles bound by rope to eyebolts that had been screwed into the living-room floor of the town house. Her tormentor, "Cody" Neal, had left her like that—naked, covered head to toe by a blanket, mouth duct-taped, surrounded by a living nightmare.

Shaking with fear, she listened for "the others" to come down the stairs. He'd said that they were up there and that if she made any noise or called out for help while he was gone, they would rape and kill her.

She had no reason to doubt him. She could still feel both the cold steel of the hunting knife he'd used to cut her clothes from her body against her skin, and the terror of the bloody piece of skull he'd placed on her bare stomach. In her mind, she could see the lifeless leg of a woman that he'd lifted from beneath a blanket over near the fireplace and the mummy-shaped object in black plastic over against a wall. He'd kicked the object, hard, and said that it was another body.

Neal had asked her if she wanted to die. She'd

told him no, but she didn't think that he was going to let her live. Not after what he'd shown her. Not after what he'd done. She was only twenty-one years old, a beautiful young woman whose life up to this point had consisted of nothing more frightening than a childhood nightmare. Now she fought to keep from crying and disturbing whoever it was that waited at the top of the stairs. She would do whatever it took to survive for as long as she could.

She'd trusted Neal when he said he wanted to show her "a big surprise" that he was going to give her roommate and his girlfriend, Beth Weeks, and then brought her to this house of horrors. They'd *all* trusted him—"Wild Bill Cody" Neal in his black cowboy hat, black duster, black shirt, and cowboy boots. The big-spender, who spread money like margarine on limousines, dinners, and parties, extravagantly tipping bartenders, drivers, and strippers to pave his way through the world. No one knew where he got all the cash. He hinted at trust funds and big business deals; others, who clung to his stories at his favorite dive bars, said that they'd heard he was a bounty hunter or even a hit man for the mob.

Scott had sensed something different about him. He'd offered her a job and a lot of money to work for him. When he added that they'd have to first fly to Las Vegas to get the OK from his lawyers, she'd hesitated and asked Weeks if she felt he could be trusted. They'd talked it over—he *was* a little mysterious—but Weeks had concluded that he would never hurt either of them.

So much for woman's intuition.

Neal seemed to be toying with Scott. After he'd

removed the piece of bone, she'd expected him to rape her. But just as he seemed to be working himself up to it, he'd stood and said that he needed to go get someone else. That's when he'd warned her about "the others" and then covered her with a blanket before leaving the town house.

To keep her mind from disintegrating into terror, she listened to the country-western music station that he'd left on the television for her entertainment. She'd counted two music videos and two commercial breaks when she heard the garage door opening again; she tensed as he came into the room. He had brought someone else with him, a female by the sound of her voice as they giggled and whispered. Scott kept as still as possible, but she couldn't quite make out what they were saying.

Scott heard the woman take a seat in the kitchen chair that she'd noticed at the foot of the mattress before Neal had covered her with the blanket. There was the sound of duct tape being pulled from a roll. After a minute, she heard Neal ask in his deep, gravelly voice, "Can you get out?" Apparently, the woman could, because there was the sound of duct tape ripping, followed by that of more tape being applied.

"That's better," she heard him say.

A few moments passed; then he asked the other woman, "So how's your day going so far?"

The woman answered, but again Scott couldn't make out what was said. She did recognize the voice as Angela Fite's, a woman she'd met once in the company of Neal at a swanky restaurant. She could understand Neal, however, when he began talking to Fite about whether she'd spoken to someone named Matt that day. Fite's answer was muffled.

Neal said something else; then Scott felt the blanket lifted from the lower half of her nude body. A hand groped at the inside of her upper thigh, causing her to recoil. Then Neal pulled the rest of the blanket off.

Fite, the mother of two young children, sat in the chair facing her. She looked frightened, but when she saw Scott, her eyes softened. "I'm sorry," Fite said, "but we're not going to get out of here alive, are we?"

Two

Karen Wilson was smitten almost as soon as the good-looking stranger had walked into the Washington, D.C., Hudson Bay Outfitters store that she managed and had opened his mouth. He wanted to hike the Appalachian Trail and needed some equipment as he was leaving that very afternoon.

She had already hiked the trail, and they spent the next hour discussing what he could expect. Many years later, she would hear unflattering physical descriptions of William Lee Neal and would say there must have been a transformation, "a sort of Dr. Jekyll and Mr. Hyde" change. Those descriptions did not fit the "Bill" she had met when he chose to approach her, rather than one of the male employees.

It wasn't that he was dressed to kill or anything, or even his long, wavy blond hair, piercing blue eyes, or engaging smile. There was just *something* about him that she couldn't quite put her finger on. Sweet, yes, and bubbly, like her. He was also into the outdoors, just like her. She could have talked to him all day; he was that . . . that charming.

The reaction surprised her. She wasn't the sort to be so easily swept off her feet by a man, even a good-looking one. A lovely twenty-two-year-old woman with waist-length strawberry blond hair, she had been born in upstate New York in 1959 to upper-middle-class parents and had attended college for two years, studying English and horticulture before the call of the wild lured her away from school. An accomplished outdoorswoman, rock climber, and cave explorer, she was the first female manager ever hired for the top-of-the-line outdoor-equipment store. She also taught kayaking and twice tried to make the U.S. Olympic canoe team, narrowly missing out by coming in second both times. She was independent, financially self-sufficient, and as tough as the wilderness treks she led as a guide. Then *he* walked in.

Unfortunately, there was a piece of equipment he wanted that her store didn't carry, so she referred him to another outfitter some distance away. He had already walked out of the store when she suddenly got the notion to offer him a ride to her competitor's place on her lunch break. She hurried outside into the sweltering heat, but he was nowhere to be seen. She drove to the other store anyway. He wasn't there. Disappointed, she sat in the parking lot for a few minutes and was about to leave, when he got off the bus in front of the store, toting his backpack.

"I was going to give you a ride," she explained lamely. He just stood there, smiling, so she told him to take care on his trip. "And when you get back, stop in and say, 'Hey,' maybe we could do a canoe trip or something." Wilson got back in her car feeling foolish. She realized she was head over heels and ruefully thought, *I'm never going to see him again. He'll go do the trail and that will be the end of it.*

She was delighted when she arrived at work the next day and found him in the store, wearing a sharp three-piece suit and sporting a new haircut. She usually only had a half hour for lunch, but he'd already talked her boss into giving her an hour. He'd decided not to go on his trip, he said, so he could take her to lunch.

When lunchtime arrived, he escorted her to a brand-new four-wheel-drive Subaru and drove her out to a country estate owned by an old couple. There, beneath two-hundred-year-old white pines, was a picnic basket already made up. They ate lunch and talked, and then there was "a surprise" waiting for her in the bottom of the basket. A silver necklace. But not just any necklace—somehow he'd found a jeweler to create a silver pendant overnight that matched the Hudson Bay Outfitters logo she'd worn on her shirt the day before. A wolf howling at the moon. He had her at that moment . . . hook, line, and sinker. *My God,* she thought, *I'm in love.*

The only problem for Wilson was that she was in an abusive relationship at the time and didn't know how to get out of it. But Neal talked her into moving back in with her parents, who were now living in Virginia, to get away from the other man so she could see him instead. Her parents loved Neal, in part because he discouraged their daughter's use of alcohol and marijuana, and he certainly seemed to treat her well. In fact, he enjoyed taking them all to dinner at the finest restaurants in the metro-Washington, D.C., area, where he seemed to know everyone from the pianist to the maître'd, who escorted them to the best table while other patrons waited in line.

Neal was charming, always a gentleman, and fond of surprises and practical jokes. Once he hid a piece of string in Wilson's spaghetti when they were visiting one of his sisters for dinner. Gagging, Wilson had spat the string out on the floor and the dog had made off with it, sending Neal into spasms of laughter. He was also in fantastic shape. Although only a little taller than Wilson, he was quick and strong, with a washboard abdomen and well-muscled arms and legs. He told her that when he was a teenager the neighbors thought he was crazy because he'd put on his backpack and, holding a canoe over his head, run around the neighborhood.

Wilson and Neal dated off and on for three years. Off and on, only because he'd disappear for months at a time, while she pined for him to return. He broke her heart every time he left, but she couldn't help herself. He seemed so perfect: smart, he could quote Thoreau, for God's sake, and read everything he could get his hands on; heroic, he let it slip that he'd been a member of the U.S. Army's Green Berets and the Alaskan Mountain Rescue Team, showing her photographs of himself on snowshoes, crossing crevasses; and ambitious, he said he owned Neal Tech, which sold alarm systems, including some he claimed to have installed in the White House. He was confident he'd be successful at whatever he put his hand to next.

His attributes seemed endless. He was also sensitive and devoted to his mother. He heartbrokenly told Wilson how his father had suffered a heart attack while driving the family car and had

died in his arms. He'd been married once but
left, he said, when he caught his wife in bed with
another man. She couldn't imagine what that
other woman had been thinking, because she
thought Neal was the sexiest man she'd ever
met—sparing no expense on romancing her,
whether it was rose petals to cover their bed, special lotions and bubble baths, or extravagant dinners, all followed by dreamy massages.

Neal seemed able to fit into any crowd. . . .
He could walk into any place and be whatever
he wanted to be. He was at home in the woods
and could talk the talk of "river people" and
wilderness guides. He was just as at ease in expensive suits and $60 haircuts at fancy gather-
ings, the sophisticate who wooed her with his
class and style. She had always dreamed of spending her life traveling, seeing new places . . . and
he was, of course, the world traveler, the man of
adventure.

He tossed around money like he made it in
his basement. She never could figure out where
he got it all. Once he told her he was a loan
officer, but she'd seen him in a security-company
truck. She didn't think it was her business to ask,
believing that the money might have something
to do with his mysterious disappearances, which
he never really explained. Or perhaps he had
generous benefactors as he seemed to know rich
people everywhere.

Once they were hiking and came upon a gorgeous log home deep in the woods, whose own-
ers he just happened to know. The couple invited
them to dinner and treated him like a long-lost
son.

Looking back many years later, she could fi-

nally see that there were signs from the very beginning that her perfect man was far from perfect. When they met, he told her he was living
with another woman, but that it was a "purely
platonic" relationship. She believed him because
she was in love, even after they went over to the
apartment one afternoon, and he told her to
duck when he saw the woman coming out of the
complex. He apparently hadn't counted on her
being there. After the coast was clear, he took
her up to the apartment and she noticed that
there was only a single king-sized bed to sleep
on. *That's some platonic relationship,* she thought,
but he told her again that there was nothing
more to it. She wanted to believe him, so she
did.

There was one quirk of his that bothered her.
They'd be walking down the sidewalk, or in a
mall or restaurant, and he'd see a woman in a
short skirt or low-cut sweater and would mutter,
"Slut." Or a pretty woman would smile at him
and he'd sneer after she passed and say something like, "She's a whore." The comments were
always made under his breath, so only Wilson
could hear, but it embarrassed her and she'd ask
him to stop. He'd just walk on as if he'd never
said a word. But the next time another woman
passed, whether it was that afternoon or a week
later, he'd be back to muttering, "Slut. Whore."

As a lover, he was imaginative and into experi-
mentation. He wanted to know her fantasies.
Had she ever thought about sex with another
woman? What about with two men? Wilson told
him, "Sure, I've thought about it; everyone has
fantasies." But that's all they were to her, fantasies that she would never have acted on.

However, there came a time when he took her to a lodge in the mountains for a romantic getaway. He didn't do drugs but knew that she liked marijuana and brought some, along with a little cocaine that he lined out. He had her slip into a negligee and opened a bottle of champagne. She was getting all warm and fuzzy, anticipating the rest of the evening, when the telephone rang.

"Who was that?" she asked after he spoke quickly into the receiver and hung up. She didn't know that anyone even knew where they were.

Neal explained that he was trying to help her fulfill a fantasy, making love to two men. He reminded her that she'd admitted thinking about it. In fact, he'd asked her what sort of fantasy man she'd want and since he was blond and blue-eyed, she'd told him, "Maybe someone with dark hair and green eyes." But it had been a joke.

Apparently not to Neal. The person on the telephone was a friend of his, "Jesse," he said, green-eyed, dark-haired, and waiting in the room next to theirs.

"My God, what are you doing?" she sputtered. She didn't want two men in her bed, only one, him. She was so angry that she started putting on her clothes, getting ready to leave. Then the telephone rang again. He picked it up and simply said, "No," and hung up.

Later he told her that she'd passed a test. "If you had said yes, our relationship would have been over," he said. "We'd have had a good time first, but it would have been over." *I passed,* she thought, *and I didn't even know I was being tested.*

There would be many more tests over the next two years, many she wouldn't do as well on. But first he talked her into moving to Houston,

Texas, with him in 1984. He said that he had a good job waiting and that's where his mother lived.

It wasn't long before the red warning flags were at full staff and flapping in the breeze. When they arrived in Houston, he had her lease their apartment in her name. He said he didn't want the woman at the rental office "knowing we're having relations." There wasn't a job waiting for him, but he made sure that she got one as soon as possible as the assistant manager at an import store.

Still, she ignored the little voice in her head, especially when, ten days after they arrived, he took her to a justice of the peace and they got married. In her mind, she was marrying her fantasy man. But she failed a second test on her wedding night, and this time she met a side of Neal she didn't know existed.

They were in their room when he said he wanted to play a game of sharing deepest, darkest secrets. He went first, admitting that he'd had sexual relations with other men. Then he asked her a question. Had she ever slept with a married man? "Yes, once," she said. "It was a mistake, and I've regretted it ever since."

Suddenly the game turned violent. He knocked her to the ground and was quickly on top of her with his hands around her throat. "Liar," he screamed in her face. "You whore!"

Wilson was terrified. *Why is he doing this?* she thought as she fought to remove his hands. *This isn't Bill.* She'd never seen him violent before. He'd talked about getting into fights with other men, but only when he had been in the right. He'd also told her that he had a black belt in karate, even had the uniform and a samurai sword, and was pretty good with his nunchakus. But he'd never exhibited a temper around her; he'd always been as sweet as pie.

Neal finally let her up. He didn't apologize; she'd done a bad thing and that's the way he saw it. He made her call the wife of the man and confess what had happened.

Under his tutelage, she soon had herself convinced that it was her fault that he'd attacked her. She'd done something wrong and that's what provoked him. She'd have to be more careful.

Life went back to normal, and Neal was his old sweet self. A few days later, he announced they were going on their "honeymoon" to a place called Canyon Lake. He'd found a romantic little cabin in the hills where they could see the lake from the front porch. She was excited that they would be spending a whole ten days he'd somehow arranged, despite their lack of money, which seemed to have dried up when they left Washington, D.C.

The night they got to the cabin, though, he wanted to play the questions game again. He asked her another question about her sexual history. A small matter really, but she should have known better than to answer him honestly. Except that's the way she'd been raised, and he'd said that for their relationship to work, they needed to always be honest with each other. So she answered truthfully, and this time found herself pinned against the wall with his hands around her throat before he pulled her to the ground and continued to throttle her. She got loose and ran from the bedroom into the living room where she hid behind the couch in a little ball. She heard him come out of the bedroom.

"Where is she?" a deep, angry voice asked. It was Neal, but a Neal she had never heard before. She quaked in fear. Not seeing her, Neal went out onto the porch and smoked a cigarette as he paced back and forth. She was obediently waiting for him, hoping he'd calmed down, when he came back in. Indeed, he acted like nothing had happened as far as what he'd done to her. It was all her fault; she had gotten what she deserved and would have to deal with the consequences.

Most of what she suffered through was emotional abuse. If she was five minutes late coming home from work, he'd want to know "who you've been fucking." If she went to the swimming pool and a man stopped to talk to her, he'd somehow know and accuse her of having an affair. He was constantly testing her, but also setting her up to fail the tests. Sometimes he wanted her to doll up when they went out for a night on the town dancing. But if another man so much as said, "Hi," and she responded, Neal would grab her by the arm, hard enough to bruise, and escort her out. "See how you are?" he'd sneer.

He'd cuss her for the smallest infractions, but it wasn't always just talk when he got angry. He'd slap her with an open hand or shove her roughly. He couldn't trust her, he'd say. But he had a quotation, something he'd read: No matter what she had done wrong, or how far she had gone down the wrong road, she could always turn back. "Turn back," he'd tell her after she'd been punished for some new transgression.

Life with Neal would always have its ups and downs. Most of the time, so long as she did what

he said and followed his rules, he was sweet Bill.
But break his rules and there'd be hell to pay.
The way he controlled all aspects of her life was
insidious. He told her how he wanted her to
dress. How to wear her hair. What to cook and
when to cook it. He moved her like a puppet,
but blinded by love, she took it as concern for
her well-being.

Of course, none of the same rules applied to
him. He came and went as he pleased, and once
he got settled in, always seemed to have plenty
of cash, though his only job was as the apartment
complex's maintenance man. That job seemed to
take him out of the apartment at all sorts of
strange hours. He'd get a call and say that he
had to go fix some woman's toilet. Later he'd
come back, snickering about how the tenant met
him in a negligee. "She just wanted to get in my
pants." She never asked if he had let her; she
always trusted him. But as far as he was concerned, she couldn't be trusted, even though she
was never unfaithful to him.

Then there was the day an envelope arrived at
their home with a pair of panties and the photograph of a beautiful woman tucked inside. "I
used to get that kind of shit all the time." He
shrugged. "It doesn't mean anything." Wilson
wondered how the woman got their address, unless he told her.

She should have left him, but she was too
close, too much in love, to understand how he
was breaking down the tough, independent
young woman she was when they had first met.
He'd taken her away from an environment where
she was secure—away from her parents, away
from her job, away from her friends. She was de-

pendent on him for everything. She had no family nearby, and he wouldn't let her have friends. She was rarely allowed to go anywhere—except to work—without him. He demeaned her every chance he got, until her self-esteem had tumbled. She couldn't leave, not when she thought that she was the one who had done wrong. If he was unhappy, then she was the one who was making him unhappy. She had to stay and make things right. *It's what you do when you really love someone,* she told herself.

Wilson couldn't figure out where Neal got his mean streak or his obsessive jealousy. His mother was as good as gold, a wonderful woman, beautiful inside and out. Mrs. Neal thought of her son as her golden child; he could do no wrong. She was the one who taught him how to act around a lady, how to be a gentleman and open doors, send flowers, write love poems.

While his mother doted on him, not everyone was fooled. Wilson's mother had changed her original opinion of Neal. She told her daughter that there was something wrong with him. "I can't put my finger on it," she said. Maybe he was just *too* nice, *too* good to be true. Her parents' misgivings were strong enough that they changed their will so that in the event of their deaths, and if their daughter split up from their son-in-law, he'd have a tough time getting his hands on her inheritance.

Even Wilson was beginning to realize that he was a natural con artist. Not just the way he could insinuate himself into any conversation, be whatever someone wanted him to be at the moment, but in little everyday ways, too. For instance, if he was hungry and lacked cash, he'd go into a

McDonald's and complain that a cheeseburger had been left out of his order and get one for free. But these were idiosyncrasies, she told herself, not something to get alarmed at.

One day one of her rings was missing when she went to look for it. The ring was a family heirloom, and she asked him repeatedly about it. Finally, he admitted that he'd taken it to a jeweler "to have it cleaned." He got it back but the initials had been ground off. The jeweler had "overcleaned" it, he said. It was obvious that the jeweler had been planning on selling the ring, but still she didn't want to admit to herself that her husband was conning her, too.

As that first year of marriage passed, the "other" William Neal was revealing himself more and more often. The comments that he made about other women in passing had continued and, if anything, were more vehement, louder, until she was worried that the women might hear. But he wouldn't stop, and if she wasn't careful, the comments were directed at her as well.

The sex began to change, too. When they were dating, their lovemaking was always pleasurable and mutually satisfying. He was always into experiments, such as body painting and photographs, but after they got to Texas, it started getting kinkier, more aggressive. Then it was "pain is good," and "it hurts when it's good." It wasn't lovemaking anymore. It was hard, angry, absentminded, almost as if she weren't a participant, or it didn't matter who was there as his partner. They had sex when he wanted, and how he wanted it. At times he would cuss her for being "a slut," slap her around, and then want to go to bed to "make up."

After a year, he decided they were going to leave Texas, which was fine with her. Neither of them liked the weather or the surroundings. They talked about using the money that they'd saved, mostly from her job, to travel up and down the East Coast looking for the next place to live.

Wilson was excited, not only for the adventure, but because she thought it might be what she and Neal needed to get their marriage back on track. Maybe if their life weren't so ordinary and stressful, they could recapture the magic. However, she should have known that nothing was going to change when he insisted before they left Texas that she be rebaptized "to cleanse your soul."

They drove a van to visit relatives and look for a place to settle down again. They stayed in Hohenwald, Tennessee, for several weeks, then moved on to New York, Vermont, and Virginia. They finally settled on Antioch, Tennessee, about fifteen minutes from Nashville. She loved it there; it was like a dream come true. Once before, when she was seventeen, she'd taken a trip down a river near Antioch; when she'd returned home, she'd told a friend that someday she'd return to Tennessee and live in a log cabin.

However, Wilson and Neal settled into a low-rent apartment, not a cabin. Then the tests and accusations resumed. They'd only been there a couple of months when Neal said that his mother had decided to move out of her home and into an apartment. He said that he had to go down and help her fix up her place to sell. He figured that he'd be gone about three weeks.

Three weeks turned into ten, and then into three months. Wilson had to take a second job and then a third to keep their place without any financial help from her husband. Neal had all kinds of excuses for why he didn't come home: his mom's place needed more work than he'd expected; then his mom's new place needed even more work. When he called, he sounded distant. She'd talk to his mother and ask her if he was all right. "Oh, honey, don't you worry about Bill, he's just fine" was the standard reply.

Wilson had no idea what could be taking him so long, but he sure seemed aware of her every move. He knew if she came home late from work. He knew if she had a bottle of beer in her hand when she answered the door. No sooner would she walk in than the telephone would ring. It would be him wanting to know where she'd been and with whom. It was eight months before he came back to Tennessee. That lasted about two weeks. Then he left a seven-page letter, front and back, listing her faults—the number one being that she couldn't be trusted. He thought that she was perfect when he married her, but she wasn't and he was sorry but he couldn't deal with it. He asked for a divorce.

She was stunned and heartbroken. Marriage was supposed to be forever, like her parents'. The next day, she was talking to the couple across the hallway when they made a startling admission. She'd just told the woman that Neal had left her when the other woman said that she'd thought Neal was a little weird. But that hadn't prevented her or her husband from keeping a journal, at his request, of Wilson's comings and goings. The woman even showed it to her—a steno pad with notations about the company she kept, her comings and goings, even what she had in her hands as she stood out in the hallway.

Wilson asked why they'd done this. The couple shrugged. Neal had befriended them but mentioned that she couldn't be trusted. So they'd agreed to spy when he asked them to keep tabs on her for him.

Two weeks after he left, he was back. He said that he loved her and wanted to make it work. She agreed. After all, she was a young woman desperately trying to salvage her marriage. She had wed for better or for worse, in sickness and in health, "till death do us part." She believed in those vows and was willing to try again.

Neal had a new plan for them. She came home one day in October 1985 to find that he'd sold all of their belongings, most of which were hers. He'd gotten rid of her climbing gear and camping equipment—thousands of dollars' worth of high-tech gear—for a fraction of what it was worth. He'd sold all of her pots and pans for $7, had gotten rid of several antiques given to her by her mother, and had given away a lot of what he couldn't sell. All she had left were a few clothes, a fifteen-inch television, and the backpack and tent she kept in her car. It was all part of a grand idea, he told her as she walked around the empty apartment in disbelief. They were going to start fresh, live in their van for a few months to save money, and then head to Colorado.

Wilson perked up at that; they'd talked about living in Colorado practically ever since they'd started going out. It was *the dream*. She didn't care about all her stuff—not much anyway—she could always get more. She cared about being with Neal, especially if they were going to Colorado. But they never left.

For the rest of October and November, they lived in the van, parked in a friend's driveway. He forbade her to go into the friend's house, except to use the rest room. She was working as a secretary and had to get herself looking presentable every morning in the cramped quarters of the van so she could go to work while he did nothing all day.

On December 1, he announced that there was a change in plans. He said that it wasn't working out. She had until January 1 to get out of the van. That's how she learned that he was divorcing her. She panicked. She had a good job, but she was going to have to find a place to live without Neal, her once-perfect man.

At the time, she couldn't understand the timing. It was only later that she realized that selling her possessions, and pocketing the money, was his way of trying to strip her of every last thing financially and emotionally. He thought that he'd force her out of Tennessee and back home to her parents. It became clear when she received the divorce papers and saw that he'd filed them before they even moved into the van that this had been his plan all along. He had never intended to go to Colorado, or anywhere else, with her.

His plan to destroy her might have worked following their first year of marriage. But there was one thing his being gone for eight months had done for her. Almost without realizing it, she had begun to take back control of her life. She was self-sufficient, paying the bills, going out with friends. Now she resolved to stay put, finding an apartment and moving in with her few possessions.

The divorce was final a few days after Christmas, 1985. The last time that she ever saw him, he found her in a girlfriend's apartment across the hall from where she lived. He demanded that the other woman leave so he could talk to his ex-wife. The other woman told him what he could do with such an order, so Wilson led him back to her place.

Even though they were divorced, he was still the same accusatory Neal. He saw that she had purchased a water bed and wanted to know why she needed it. She told him that she needed a place to sleep, "and what business is it of yours?" Finally, he got down to the business that he'd come to discuss: he wanted her to leave town; she was cramping his style.

Wilson refused; she had little else, but she had herself back. She said that she wasn't budging. If anyone was leaving, it would have to be him. He stormed out, parting with one chilling prediction: "I'm going to fuck over every woman in my path. You all ain't nothing but a bunch of whores."

She didn't hear from him again until March. He called her from Texas and, more shocking than anything he'd done to date, apologized. All that time he was in Texas, he said, he'd been living with another woman . . . apparently the same woman she could now hear yelling at him in the background. "The divorce wasn't your fault," he said. But the apology was only half-hearted and it was clear he really did blame her. "You know I put you on a pedestal. . . . You were my perfect little bird," he said. "Then when I found out you weren't perfect, I didn't know what to do. I couldn't trust you."

So, she thought, *the first test I failed on our wed-*

ding night destroyed my marriage. She had never given him a reason not to trust her, had never been unfaithful. All she had done was fail tests she had been set up to fail. He'd said that he was sorry, but she'd always wonder what his real motive was. Was it because he really did love her at one time, or at least thought he did? Or did he call her to apologize as a way to hurt the woman who was yelling at him in Texas?

For three years, Wilson mourned the loss of her marriage. There were times when she wished he'd come back, not knowing if she'd have the strength to turn him away if he did. At the same time, whenever someone inquired about her past and she told them, she'd add, "If you ever run into a man named William Lee Neal, turn and walk the other way."

It was a long time before she would trust another man enough to let him get close to her. She had a friend, Fred, who gradually let her know that he cared for her. He wasn't overly romantic, nor did he live life on the edge. He was soft and gentle, shy and yet strong, a man who didn't need to beat his chest. With him she felt safe and loved. They got married and had a daughter in 1989.

However, just because she was through with Bill Neal, it didn't mean that he was through with her. Every now and then, there'd be a telephone call from him. Even if she moved, he found her. She got unlisted telephone numbers, changed them seven times over the next nine years, but still the phone would ring and it would be him. Finally, she quit trying to hide. He was going to find her if he wanted. More frightening, he seemed to know as much about her as ever. She'd get a new car and he'd call and tell her that he liked her choice. He was letting her know that he was still keeping tabs on her, still in control.

Meanwhile, Neal seemed to be going through some pretty rough times. He often sounded drunk when he called. He had a bad cough that never seemed to get better. She stayed close to his family, who kept her updated on what they knew of his whereabouts and activities, though he was secretive with them, too. His mother told her that she had scolded him "for losing the best thing you ever had," and she continued to treat Wilson like a daughter.

Through them, Wilson learned that he'd married again, to another Karen—Karen Boxer. He'd apparently taken her, too, for her money, prompting calls to Wilson from police investigators looking for Neal. He'd divorced a third time and then married a fourth, this time a young stripper named Jennifer Tate.

Apparently, he was hanging out in Denver, Colorado, bars a lot, acting like something out of a Wild West show. He told her that he'd even legally changed his name to William "Cody" Neal, but that he was known in the bars and strip joints as Wild Bill Cody. She had to laugh at this latest reincarnation; he'd never been a cowboy, not a real one.

The calls stopped for a time. Then her parents died, first her dad and then her mother, and he called soon afterward. He was well aware that she stood to inherit a considerable amount of money, and now he wanted some of it. But her parents had put the money in a trust, and while she received lump sums from it on a regular basis—a fact he seemed to know—it was tough to put her hands on the kind of money he asked for. Otherwise, she would have still found it difficult to stand up to Neal and his stories. He'd try different tactics to get money out of her. Once it was that the Mafia was after him; he said that he owed the mob money and if he didn't pay it back, a hit man was going to take him out. She was racked with guilt. *God, if I don't give him the money, he might die.* But she didn't give him the money, and he managed to stay alive. It didn't stop him from trying a different story though.

Only once did she hear again from the man she had loved and married. His mother died in October 1995, and he called distraught and needing a sympathetic shoulder. He told Wilson that he loved her, that he had always loved her. She had to admit she felt the old twinge when he said that. No matter what he'd done to her, there was always that one last shred of some memory that he could use to make her cry.

She expressed her sympathy for his loss. She had truly loved his mom like her own. It was nice to be talking to plain old Bill, not some stranger who called himself Cody. But there was no going back, she told him. Maybe someday, when they were both sixty, she said, they'd meet again and talk about old times. Until then, she wished him the best of luck.

The last time she heard from Neal, he called out of the blue asking for money again. He said that he needed it so he could divorce his fourth wife, Jennifer. Once he had the divorce, he'd be free and hinted that maybe they should hook up again. She didn't give him the money.

When she called one of his sisters, she learned that he had already divorced Jennifer Tate. He was just trying to con her again. This time Wilson pulled a con of her own. She told her new husband, Fred, that William Neal had died. She didn't want to have to explain the real reason why a telephone call would put her in a bad mood. For her, Neal had told her his last lie and really was dead, at least to her heart.

Three

September 1992, Denver, Colorado

She was just eighteen-years-old and a topless dancer when he came into her life and swept her off her feet with his money and style. All the other dancers at the club wanted to be with the charming guy in the black cowboy hat, who spent lavishly to keep beautiful young women surrounding him at his table. He tipped everyone— the doorman, the bartenders, the strippers—so well that every time he walked in, they played "his" song, "Strokin'," a randy R & B song by Clarence Carter that was censored on the airwaves when released in 1990.

Although a lovely young woman, Jennifer Tate never thought that she'd have a chance of getting to go out with him. She was petite—her nickname was "Baby Half-pint"—and she didn't think that she compared to the "supermodels" who fastened onto the man they called "Wild Bill Cody" as soon as he came in the door. But on her nineteenth birthday, September 29, 1992, he strolled over to the stage where she was dancing and laid out $1,000 in $1 bills. Then he asked her out.

Tate had made it a policy not to date customers. If "date" was what you'd call what most of them wanted. Usually their line was something like, "I'll give you five hundred dollars to go to bed with me." But Cody was different. He was never so crude as to suggest a simple exchange of money for sex. He was much more subtle than that.

So she broke her rule and went out with him. He picked her up and took her to a Chinese restaurant, a type of food that she didn't like, but it didn't matter because she did like the way that he talked to her. She knew from dressing-room gossip that he was good at getting the girls to sit down and tell him their life stories. With dancers, that always meant some sob tale: life was rough, or they had family problems, or they were insecure about their looks. But, as Tate discovered, he always knew the right words to say. He made her feel like she was an angel from heaven in his eyes. She *wanted* to be with him.

Like many of the other girls, Tate had her own hard-luck story. Her father had walked out on her mother and her when she was three. Then there'd been a succession of other men in her mother's life, many of them abusive, until she was six and her mother remarried.

Tate didn't like dancing or the men who wanted to buy her affection. Nor did she like the lifestyle that went along with strip clubs; most of the other girls were into cocaine, something she associated with a bad childhood. She wanted nothing more than to be married; then there'd be no more dancing. She'd have a man who loved her for something other than sex. They'd settle down in a little house and raise their children in a stable, healthy environment.

Two days after her nineteenth birthday, she found herself hoping that this handsome man might be the answer to her dreams. He was older than she was, but he acted like he owned the world. Besides, she thought he looked real good in a tight pair of blue jeans.

At dinner that night, he seemed aware of her fondest dreams, as though he could read her mind. He challenged her to use her chopsticks to pick up an ice cube from his glass. He said that if she could do it on the first attempt, he was going to fly them both to Las Vegas to get married that night. She was disappointed that it took her two tries.

Two days after their first date, she moved in with him. For all his extravagance in public, he lived in a tiny apartment with mismatched furniture, including two reclining chairs but no couch in the living room. She didn't care. His money had attracted her attention, but it was Wild Bill Cody she wanted.

He was part owner of a security company, Dynamic Control Systems, which is where she thought he made his money. It had to be a good business. He always had a new car and continued to spread cash around on partying like fertilizer on a farm.

Cody was very romantic. He'd fix her bubble baths and spread rose petals on their bed. He bought her nice clothes, including sexy little negligees, and liked to take her out, spending wildly on their nights on the town. His place was her place, he said, with one exception, a closet that he kept locked and she was not to go into.

He was secretive about his past life in general. He hardly mentioned his family, except to note

that he was very close to his mother. But he did
tell her that he'd been married three times before; he even bragged how he put his third wife
in the "loony bin" after she tried to kill him. He
also said he'd been in the army, a member of
the elite Airborne Rangers, who taught him the
wilderness survival skills that would allow him to
live in any type of country indefinitely.

Tate used birth control and he used condoms,
but she was soon pregnant anyway. It wasn't long
after she found out that she first saw another
side to the Wild Bill Cody she loved.

A gay friend asked her to go out to dinner
with him. She knew Cody was a little jealous; he
didn't even want her to see her old girlfriends.
He warned her often that all that other men
wanted her for was sex. She thought it would be
OK to spend the evening with a gay man.

But she didn't know that William Neal didn't
like gays, or blacks, or Hispanics for that matter.
When she got home, she found that he'd packed
all of her possessions into two garbage sacks and
was kicking her out. Nineteen years old and two
months pregnant, with nowhere to go, she
begged him for forgiveness. She said she would
do anything to make him happy.

Angry, he drove her down to his office at Dynamic Control. He made her sit in a chair in the
middle of the room and began the inquisition.
While she was out that night, he'd gone through
her things and found a list of the boys she'd slept
with in high school. It was just a list and she'd
had no contact with those lovers since. He told
her it was proof that she was no good.

"Don't you know how this hurts me?" he
screamed. Then he said something that didn't

make sense at the time. "I was molested by a preacher when I was young!" he yelled, and she had just betrayed him again. "You're a slut. . . . A whore."

Tate was terrified. He didn't seem like the same man. She cried, but he responded by frightening her further. "If you're scared now, you don't know how evil I can be," he snarled. "You don't know meaning of scared."

After he was through lecturing her, he took her back. All of her high school yearbooks and diaries disappeared, never to be seen again, and the relationship was never the same. "You don't know meaning of scared" became a favorite saying, and Tate thought of his office as "the punishing zone" because he took her there to berate her whenever she'd "been bad."

Yet, he could behave anyway he wanted. He liked to go to The Stampede, a country-western bar, where he'd throw money over the railing onto the dance floor below and laugh as he watched people scramble to pick up the cash. But that's not all he liked at that bar. While patrons were picking up bills below, he'd have his hand up their waitress's skirt in full view of pregnant Jennifer Tate.

She had quickly learned that Cody's sexuality wasn't all bubble baths and romantic evenings. His favorite television programming was pornography, which he insisted she watch with him. She also learned fairly quickly that he was still seeing some of the other dancers she thought she'd won him away from, though he would always deny that he had been unfaithful. If she complained about his dalliances, or anything else for that matter, he'd kick her out, force her to move back in with her mother. Sometimes he'd leave her there for weeks before calling to tell her she could come home.

Still, he married her when she was five months pregnant, at which time he demanded that she stop dancing. It was all that she had ever wanted, and she hoped that with the exchange of vows, he would trust her more, realize that she was his and his alone. However, the pattern of accusations and kicking her out of the apartment continued.

When she was nine months pregnant, he kicked her out again. Lonely, she agreed to go "cruising" the main boulevard of the town with her sister. They were stopped in the middle of the street when a young man ran out and gave her sister a kiss. For once, Cody's spying failed him, but only by degrees. She'd only been home for a few minutes that night when he called and demanded to know who *she* had been kissing. Fortunately in this case, he somehow had photos of the kiss, which demonstrated that the recipient was her sister. Obviously, he was having her followed.

It only got worse. He gave her $1,000-per-week "spending money," but she wasn't allowed to go anywhere unless chaperoned by himself or one of his sisters who lived in Denver. She wasn't to go grocery shopping or to the laundry on her own. Break the rules and it was a quick trip to the "punishment zone," or pack her bags for her mother's house.

There were always more rules. She was to leave him alone at work. She wasn't to question where he went at all hours of the night, though he'd often come home at 3:00 A.M. or later, drunk and accusing her of sleeping around.

Tate, a bright, quick-witted young woman, knew there was something very wrong with her marriage. But she was pregnant, and she'd always promised herself that no child of hers would grow up without a father. Cody knew that; he'd taken great pains at the beginning of their relationship to learn such things and used it to his advantage.

When she went into labor on July 24, 1993, Cody wasn't around. She'd called him only to be told, "Goddamn it, I'm working." So she'd gone to the hospital with her sister and her mom. Cody showed up about 10:00 P.M. She still hadn't delivered, so he went to a bar and wasn't seen the rest of the night. He did pick her and their child up the next morning. He took them home and left again.

The child gave Cody more power over her. He constantly threatened to take their daughter and disappear if Tate didn't do as she was told. Even when she was home with the infant, he was sure she was seeing other men. Once she took a nap in the morning and accidentally knocked the telephone off the hook. The next thing she knew, there was the sound of their front door being kicked in. Then he was standing over her in the bedroom, sure he'd caught her in the act.

No matter how hard she tried, Cody wouldn't let her be the wife that she wanted to be. She wasn't allowed to cook dinner. Those occasions when he did eat at home, he just wanted to order pizza. The family life that she had envisioned never materialized.

The romance was definitely gone as well, replaced by sex on command, which he'd indicate he wanted by his code phrase "potty for Daddy."

Sex was such a paradox with Cody, and he was constantly testing her. He'd ask what she'd do if he wanted her to have sex with another man. She'd say she didn't want to. "But what if it would make me happy?" he'd ask. Fortunately, she saw the trap. Making him happy was one thing, but she knew if she gave in, he'd have thrown one of his temper tantrums and called her a whore.

Then there was the occasion he took her to an adults-only swingers motel. He insisted that she watch the videos piped into the room so that she could learn "to give a proper blow job" and be instructed on how to masturbate. After the videos, they went out to the pool area where another man touched her leg suggestively. She told Cody, but he said not to worry about it, "that sort of thing happens all the time here." She grew more uncomfortable when other people started having sex in front of her. She was glad that Cody didn't object when she insisted on going back to their room.

In the room, he was his old sweet, sexy self. Then he told her he had "a surprise." First he insisted on blindfolding her; then he tied her hands above her head. She wanted to make him happy, so she went along with the moment, even when he suggested that he open the curtains to the outside so that others could watch. He had obviously been to the motel before as he explained "the code": open curtains meant "feel free to watch"; an open door meant join in. She said the open curtains were OK, but she didn't want to have sex with anybody else.

He began to make love to her and then paused. Then she felt someone had entered her and it wasn't her husband. Tate started kicking and demanding that Cody get whoever it was off her. The other man seemed as confused as she was angry. "I thought it was OK," he apologized.

Cody told the man to leave. He then tried to comfort his wife and finally took her home. The next day, however, he kicked her out of the apartment. He said he needed time to work and she needed to go see her family, but she knew the real reason.

Cody's increasingly aggressive sexuality troubled her. More alarming was the day she left their daughter with him while she went on one of the few outings she was allowed with a friend. When she came home, everything seemed fine. Cody said that he'd given their daughter a bath and then put her to bed. It wasn't until the next day when she tried to wash the child herself that a red flag went up in her mind. The child, who had always enjoyed "tub time" before, suddenly fought getting into the bathtub, crying and screaming.

Tate didn't want to think that Cody was capable of molesting his own child, but she mentioned it to one of his sisters anyway. The sister told her to be careful. In the mid-1980s, Cody had come under suspicion in a case in New York where a little girl had been abducted from a gas station, raped, and killed. He'd been in the vicinity at the time and questioned by the FBI. His sister understood that he'd been dropped from the list of suspects, but what she didn't tell Tate was that he had molested another little girl when he was young. She just cautioned Tate to be careful about leaving her brother alone with the child.

Shortly before Thanksgiving Day, 1994, Tate finally had it with her husband. She hadn't seen him in three days. He'd left her and her daughter without food or diapers, and of course she wasn't allowed to go get them. Then he called about 3:00 A.M. She could hear him talking to another woman in the background.

"Don't forget to wear a condom," she yelled. Right away she knew it was a mistake to challenge him like that.

Clearly angry, he yelled that he was on his way home. She was scared to death and called the police so that she would be safe to pack her things. He arrived, but with the police present he couldn't do anything except glare and refuse to let her have a car to leave in. The police called a cab for her.

For once, Cody was in a predicament. He'd invited his mother up from Texas for Thanksgiving so that she could meet his wife and baby for the first time. He called Tate and asked if she would forgive him and come to dinner for his mother's sake. She relented. "Just act like everything is OK between us," he said when he picked her up.

Tate fell in love with his mom. The old woman welcomed her with open arms and doted over her grandchild. But Cody's older sister, Sharon, who knew what was going on between the couple, took her down to the basement of her home and lectured Tate about being a better wife. Tate knew better than to argue; next to his mother, Cody loved his sister Sharon best.

When Thanksgiving dinner was over, Cody

took Tate back to her mother's house, where she remained until May 1995. Not that he lost track of her. He must have had someone watching her because he knew everything she did, whether it was shopping or going out with her sister. His calls, however, were always mushy and romantic. "I miss you, Half-pint. I love you, Half-pint." She thought that maybe he'd seen the error of his ways and they might try to make their marriage work, but he said he wasn't ready for her to come home yet.

In May he finally asked her back. They even moved into a new apartment. He told her that he'd narrowly escaped going to prison while she was gone. He'd embezzled close to $70,000 from Dynamic Control Systems and had been forced to hand over his share of the company to his partners to avoid prosecution.

She was more concerned with his womanizing. As they packed up the old apartment, he'd allowed her to look in the locked closet for the first time. It was stuffed with army duffelbags, but she couldn't tell what they contained. The only thing he showed her were hundreds of photographs and letters from other women. She knew he was doing it to make her jealous, but he insisted that he'd been faithful throughout their marriage.

One day a blond woman who looked to be in her forties came to the apartment looking for Cody. She told Tate, who'd answered the door, that she would wait outside to speak to him. Cody seemed real nervous when Tate told him a woman was waiting for him; he practically ran to the door and ushered the other woman quickly back to her car.

It was obvious the woman was her husband's lover. Angry, Tate swore at him when he returned and said she would never sleep with him again. She left, taking only her daughter and a diaper bag. She had no job, no money . . . but at last she was through with Wild Bill Cody. She left her marriage for her own sake, but even more for their daughter's. The necessity for leaving him was driven home one day when a neighbor of her mother's dropped by. He was wearing a black cowboy hat like the one Cody wore. Her daughter began to sob. "No, don't make my mommy cry."

The irony was that Cody divorced her in March 1996. She didn't see him again until that July. It was their daughter's third birthday, and the little girl had decided she wanted to see her daddy. In all that time, he'd attempted to make contact only twice: he'd sent two cards, one for Valentine's Day and one for her birthday. Of the two years between their daughter's birth and their divorce—if Tate totaled every minute, every hour, every day, that Cody spent with their child, it would amount to perhaps two months. In all of the photographs that she had of him and their daughter, he had an expression on his face that seemed to say, "Hurry up and get this over with." Only when he was in public, trying to impress people, had he ever acted like the doting father. But Tate told her daughter they'd go see him.

She found Cody at a bar called Shipwreck's, where she knew he spent a lot of time. He was surrounded by women and a few men, holding drunken court. He acted glad to see Tate and made a big show of taking his daughter around, even referring to Tate as "my wife."

After she left, Tate felt good about how the meeting went. She hoped that things would work out so that her daughter would grow up knowing her father. Maybe, with the passage of time, she and Cody would be friends again.

Then she received a letter from him. It warned her: "Stay the fuck out of my life." He said he didn't want his friends to know she even existed.

Tate did as he requested, happy to walk away with nothing more than full custody of her daughter and his promise to pay $350 a month in child support. Otherwise, she thought she'd seen and heard the last of Wild Bill Cody Neal.

Four

"You've just got to meet this cowboy."

Rebecca Holberton smiled at her friend's insistence at setting her up with the smiling man in the tight black T-shirt and even tighter blue jeans. They were at an outdoor party, and she didn't really know most of the people present. At forty-two years old, she had not expected to meet someone romantically, being a little on the shy side when it came to men since her divorce a couple of years earlier. She wasn't seeing anyone in particular and lived on her own in a town house she'd recently purchased on West Chenango Drive in unincorporated Jefferson County, a large, mostly rural area that encompassed a half-dozen bedroom communities northwest of Denver.

The man in question was a little on the short side, but she had to admit that he had cheerful blue eyes beneath the black Stetson he wore, and a sexy voice—sort of a low, rumbling western twang. "Just call me Cody," he said when they were introduced.

Forty years old, William Lee Neal was no longer the young outdoorsman he'd been when he met his second wife, Karen Wilson, in Washington, D.C., or even the free-spending patron of the strip club where he met his fourth wife, Jennifer Tate, and where all the girls and bartenders knew him as Wild Bill Cody.

He'd developed a paunch, and the muscles of his youth were soft with alcohol and disuse; he had a persistent cough from the cigarettes he chain-smoked. But he still carried himself like he owned the world, and his tongue was as glib as ever, maybe more so from the years of practice. He wore his hair long beneath the hat, which, he'd tearfully point out to any listening female, had been given to him by his dear departed mother. "The only thing I have left that's from her," he'd say.

Holberton thought he was cute and he certainly came on strong with his charm that afternoon; soon they were seeing each other every day. In many ways, he seemed like the perfect man. He was a great listener and offered what seemed to be good advice on everything from her finances to remodeling her town house.

He was sensitive, too, particularly when it came to his young daughter, who his former wife—an "evil," unfaithful stripper, he said—kept from him. His descriptions of his battle to win custody of the child would bring him to tears, as would any mention of his mother.

Cody, as he wanted to be called, romanced her with roses and back rubs. Always the gentleman, he opened doors and lit her cigarettes as fast as she could get them out of the pack.

There was also an air of mystery and wealth about him. He sometimes painted houses for a living, but said that was just to get by while he waited for a trust fund to be released to him. The fund was currently tied up in the Las Vegas court system but, he said, when he eventually got his hands on the money, he'd be rich beyond her imagination. He sometimes hinted that the money had something to do with his mob connections, or "The Family," as he referred to them, warning her that she had to keep that knowledge a secret. Or else.

It just added to his allure and she'd fallen for him. He moved in with her after a few weeks of dating.

Holberton wasn't the only one convinced that Neal was something more than an underemployed house painter. When he divorced Jennifer Tate in March, he'd claimed to be $51,000 in debt, listed an old truck and $4 as his only assets, and described himself as an "unemployed alarm technician." However, around the dive bars he frequented, he talked as if he were a bounty hunter, or some heard he'd once been a hit man for the mob. He cultivated the image by always dressing in black—from the crown of his Stetson to his shirts, with maybe a break in the motif for blue jeans. On cooler days, he also sported a long black duster that reached down to his black cowboy boots.

He told a lot of stories, such as having been one of the army's elite Airborne Rangers. He seemed to know what he was talking about. At least that's what the regulars at the bars thought who listened to him spin his tales as he sipped his favorite drink, rum and Coke, and bought rounds for his audiences. Not everyone heard the same story, which rather than identifying him as a liar, only enhanced his mystique.

The money helped. He seemed to have plenty of it around, too—$50 tips for a few drinks or a haircut, limousines, wild parties at local hotels. Depending upon which story one heard, the money came from a trust fund or his shady past. One story even combined the two: Years before, he was supposed to kill a wealthy man in Las Vegas for The Family, but he decided to spare the man. The intended victim was so grateful, he'd set up a trust fund for Neal.

Not everyone bought his act. Plenty knew he was a con artist almost as soon as they heard him speak; but being a "liar and a strange bird," as one bartender would later describe him to the police, wasn't against the law. He ignored or avoided those who saw him for what he was. . . . They were of no use to him.

In September 1997, Holberton and Neal went to Las Vegas to meet up with her best friend and former sister-in-law, Tammy. Tammy wasn't impressed. He struck her as the kind of guy who lived by mooching off others. He did seem to have some connections in Las Vegas, because Holberton confided that they were getting their room for free.

Still, if Rebecca was happy, then Tammy was happy for her and didn't worry much over Cody. That is, not until Holberton called a few months later and said she might be contacted by her insurance company. Apparently, she'd had some expensive jewelry stolen on the trip, though she hadn't mentioned it at the time. Now she was warning Tammy that the insurer might call to verify if Holberton had once owned the jewelry. After they got off the telephone, Tammy wondered if Cody had anything to do with its "disappearance."

Neal had plenty of drinking buddies among the men at the bars, but not many who thought of themselves as his friend. Instead, he surrounded himself with the women, who gravitated to his old-fashioned manners, shadowy past, and money. He certainly knew how to win them over. He frequently ordered flowers—always longstemmed red roses—from Beverly Wise, a local florist, and had them sent to various dancers at strip clubs. The florist thought he was such a polite man, who always paid with cash. Even she was somewhat taken in by his air of mystery, such as the time he asked her to deliver two arrangements of roses to a hotel room.

"Who for?" she teased.

Neal smiled back. "Nobody in particular," he said. "I'm just gonna go out, find a girl, and let her think I did it all for her."

The only problem with Neal's generosity was the money wasn't his. It came from other people. Some from his former business partners, but mostly from women he could seduce out of their savings. Rebecca Holberton was one of those women.

When she met Neal, Holberton was leading a quiet, uneventful life. She'd once been married to an airline pilot, Rodney Holberton, but they divorced with no children. For twenty-three years, she'd worked for US West telephone company, where she was considered a well-liked, exemplary employee, though her friends at work worried about her occasional bouts with depression. Most of her career had been spent in Portland, Oregon, before transferring to the Denver office in 1995, in part to get a fresh start on life.

She hadn't lived at the town house for long before Neal moved in, which might have had something to do with why her neighbors thought of her as distant. She rarely returned greetings and never wanted to stop and chat or introduce her new boyfriend, who also kept to himself. Not long after the man in the cowboy hat moved in, butcher paper went up on the inside windows of their town house, as if preparing to paint the interior.

Two years later, the paper was still up, but time was running out for Neal. The romance with Holberton had faded quickly enough from their relationship, until sex was no longer part of it. They were more like roommates. He came and went as he pleased, often spending days away from the town house. She had to have been aware that he was seeing other women, though it's hard to tell if she was hurt more by that or by the realization that her "perfect man" had taken her for nearly every penny she owned.

Somehow over a two-year period, she'd let him borrow more than $60,000, much of it she'd had to borrow against her credit. Some of it was supposedly for his custody battle; another portion of it was for business ventures that he promised would make them both a lot of money when they matured. They just never seemed to reach that point, and the legal battle for his trust fund—with which he promised to pay her with interest—seemed to go on and on with no end in sight.

By June 1998, she'd had enough. She was starting a new position at the telephone company on

July 6 and was excited at the prospect, circling the date on her desk calendar. She told a friend that she was going to get Cody Neal out of her home and out of her life. But she wanted her money back first.

Holberton confronted Neal and threatened to go to the police. On June 29, he surprised her by announcing that he was finally going to be able to pay her back. His trust fund had been released by the courts. As a measure of how certain he was, he urged her to write nearly $56,000 in checks to pay her creditors. The money to cover the checks would be in her account the next day, he said, when he would also give her "a surprise" to demonstrate his gratitude for her patience. That was in addition to taking her to Las Vegas for an all-expense-paid holiday before she started her new job.

The next morning, Neal rose early and drove to a building-supplies store. He'd been thinking of this plan for a couple of weeks and so he knew exactly what he needed. He already had a large footlocker back at the town house and a new circular saw. Now he moved quickly through the aisles picking up Lava soap—good for scrubbing almost anything off skin—four large eyebolts, nylon rope, duct tape, and . . . He went to the area of the store where the various axes, sledgehammers, and mauls waited. He tried the heft of several before settling on a seven-and-a-half-pound splitting maul—half ax and half sledgehammer—with a long wooden handle. Just right.

When Neal got back to the town house on West Chenango Drive, he pulled into the garage and closed the door. He left the maul in the truck to scout out the situation. Holberton was up, though still dressed in her nightgown.

"Ready for your surprise?" he asked with a smile. He noted her excitement; she was "filled with joy and happiness," he would later say. He led her to a chair that he'd placed on the plywood floor of the living room—she'd planned to have it carpeted soon—facing the sliding glass door that led to the backyard. He then fetched a briefcase and placed it on her lap. It was heavy, as though it held tens of thousands of dollars. He'd wanted the weight of it to be a distraction, though in actuality it held only newspapers.

Neal went to the kitchen and returned with a bottle of champagne. Popping the cork, he poured them both a glass and toasted their new fortunes, their new lives. Setting his glass down, he picked up a blanket, which he said he wanted to place over her head for her "surprise." She protested that it would mess up her hair, but relented at his insistence.

Placing the blanket carefully over her blond hair, he announced, "I have to go get something in the garage. Be right back!" He walked quickly to the garage and picked up the maul. Returning to the living room, he noticed that his little white kitten was strolling about, rubbing against Rebecca's legs. He raised the maul, his eyes fixed on the center top of Holberton's head.

A pause. A heartbeat. A breath. Then the maul whistled down in an arc, the sledgehammer side crushing into the woman's skull. Her hands flew up involuntarily to her head as Neal quickly swung the maul again like a man driving in a spike. As he struck again and again, and she pitched out of the chair, he noticed that her head was becoming sloppy and that a rip had appeared in the cloth through which blood and brain matter seeped.

At last Neal was finished. He turned and walked a few steps over to a hall closet, where he left the bloody maul. Going back to his victim, he removed the blanket and placed Holberton's head in a plastic bag to catch some of the blood. He lashed her arms and legs with rope, and then encased his victim in black plastic lawn bags, which he bound with the duct tape until she looked like a mummy. He then dragged the body over to a wall to the right of the chair.

Turning, Neal noticed a two-inch piece of skull lying on the floor, bloody blond hair still attached. Using the paper from an ice-cream bar, he picked up the bone and carried it to the kitchen. The first part of his plan was complete. He'd given them fair warning, told them all: "Anybody who believes me deserves to get fucked."

Well, now they'd believe him. But there wasn't time to rest on his laurels, he had to go visit Candace Walters and put the second part of his plan in motion. As he left the room, he noticed his kitten. . . . Poor little thing, her belly hadn't come off the floor since his attack on Rebecca. *She knows who the biggest predator is,* he thought.

Five

Neal held the blanket up to cover Candace Walters. She was sitting in the chair where just a few days earlier he'd murdered Rebecca Holberton, but Candace had not noticed the mummylike object wrapped in black plastic, partly covered by a scrap of carpet, over against a wall. If she did, he was prepared to tell her it was just some remodeling materials; he'd already warned her that the place was a mess.

Happy and excited, Candace balanced a briefcase on her lap as she waited for her "surprise" in the pretty white sundress she'd worn for their trip to Las Vegas. "No, Cody," she complained, refusing the blanket. "I don't want to mess up my hair."

Neal shrugged. He knew better than to try to get the forty-eight-year-old woman to do something she didn't want to do. Besides, she was already suspicious of him. So he gently draped the blanket around her shoulders. "Well, promise to keep your eyes closed," he said as he walked behind her toward the closet where he kept the maul.

They'd met a few days after Christmas the year

before, at a hotel where she worked as a bartender. He was charismatic and generous, tipping her extravagantly for every drink or courtesy. More than that, he was caring and such a good listener; after she got off work, they sat in a booth talking all night.

Cody, as he'd introduced himself, was mysterious about where all that money he threw around came from. But, she told her daughter, Holly, he was obviously a very sensitive man who'd almost cried as he talked about the court battle he was waging to gain custody of his young daughter. He'd invited her to a New Year's Eve party that he was throwing at the hotel. She'd attended and had a great time with him.

Like Holberton, Candace Walters had once been married. But she and her husband had divorced some twenty-five years earlier, shortly after moving to Colorado with their infant daughter, Holly. They'd remained friends—in fact, when her father died shortly after the divorce and left her a small inheritance of a few thousand dollars, she'd used part of it to buy her ex-husband a household's worth of furniture since he'd left her everything in the divorce—but she'd had few committed relationships since then. When the last one ended some four or five years earlier, she'd told her daughter, "I think I'll just stay away from men."

Holly didn't mind; she'd loved having the bulk of her mother's attention since earliest childhood. She'd lived with her mother until she was twenty-three, when she moved to Seattle. They'd talked nearly every day, but the separation had been too hard and Holly had moved back and into the same apartment complex as her mother.

When Holly moved to a larger complex, Candace followed two months later and moved in next door.

The older they got, the closer they grew. They particularly loved taking nature walks in the foothills, sharing their days and their dreams. Walters didn't have much in the way of material possessions, but her daughter loved listening to her philosophy about living life as fully as possible. Her dreams were simple: a small house of her own with a yard where she could keep a dog, and have enough free time to do the things she loved . . . like hiking with her daughter or just sitting around reading together, content just to be near.

When Candace glowed while talking about the New Year's Eve party and her new boyfriend, Holly asked what she found attractive about him. "He makes me laugh" was the reply.

Holly accepted that, though she was surprised at how quickly the relationship blossomed over the next few weeks. Still, anyone who could make her mother so happy couldn't be all bad, she reasoned. She was more concerned about getting her mother out of the bartending business; she didn't like the hours and there was no telling whom she might meet. Shortly after the New Year, Holly, who owned a successful mortgage company, asked her mother to come work for her.

In the meantime, Candace Walters was spending an increasing amount of time and energy with Cody Neal. If she wasn't out with him, she was talking to him on the telephone.

Holly was growing wary of the man with all the tall tales and seemingly endless supply of money.

She knew her mother could take care of herself; she'd run away to Chicago to live on the streets for a time when she was fourteen, back in the days of Flower Power and hippies, and had turned out just fine. But she could also be extremely trusting and gave a lot of herself when she committed to a relationship, and she expected a lot in return.

Holly knew that despite her mother swearing off men, she was tired of being alone. And here came this guy, Mr. Cody Neal, offering the moon. She knew her mother well enough to know that it wasn't the money he spent so freely but his presence and the way he communicated that held the attraction.

Holly worried about where this was all leading. For instance, there was the small matter of his supposed occupations. Early on, he'd told her mother that he was involved in real estate in Las Vegas. Then her mother came home with a story about him maybe being a bounty hunter, which was soon trumped by his having once been a hit man for a mob family. When Holly expressed concern about that bit of information, her mother assured her that—if it was even true, and she wasn't convinced—he'd retired from the killing profession years ago. Even then, he'd only killed people who deserved it . . . bad men who crossed the family.

He also claimed he'd made $50 million dealing real estate in Hawaii. It was an enormous amount of money, but Holly knew from her own business that achieving such a sum in that market was feasible, if unlikely. He certainly acted like he had money—once even telling her mother that he had to fly to New York City for the weekend to look into purchasing rare gems. Her mother told her it was nothing for him to leave a $20 tip for a single drink or stuff a $100 bill into a bellhop's hand.

Unfortunately, most of his money seemed to be tied up in a trust account. A judge had frozen the account while he was in a custody battle with his former wife for his young daughter. So sometimes, he explained, he had cash flow problems. It was during one of those times that he asked to borrow $1,500 from Candace. He was very mysterious about what he was going to do with the money, but said he needed her to ask for $1 bills in bundles of twenty.

Candace Walters didn't have much in the way of savings, and what she did have, she had set aside so that she could go back to school and someday buy that dream home. But she loaned him the money and was relieved when he repaid it two days later and earlier than he said he would. She thought that showed that he could be trusted.

Holly wasn't so sure. Her mother was happier than she'd ever seen her, and she didn't want to jeopardize her mother's relationship with Cody, but still she took down the license plate of the truck he drove . . . just in case.

She grew more alarmed when she learned in March that her mother had loaned him $6,000. Candace said he needed it for his battle to gain custody of his daughter. His ex-wife was a greedy stripper who wanted $300,000 to release custody of the child to him. He was willing to pay it, but his money was tied up in the trust fund. In the meantime, he had a team of lawyers he had to pay to get his money and his child. It had been absolutely heartbreaking when he tearfully told her that he believed that his daughter had been raped by a male friend of his ex-wife's. He was so upset that he talked of killing the man.

By April, however, Candace Walters was troubled about the course of her relationship. On the one hand, she loved Cody and wanted to help him save his daughter, but he'd also borrowed nearly every cent she had in the world and made no mention of when she might be repaid. She began asking him about her money. He told her that he expected the trust fund would soon be unfrozen by the courts, but there was another problem of people wanting to get their hands on his money and he had to be careful. "The Family," he said, also thought that his own lawyer might be leaking information to his ex-wife's lawyer. Cody said he might have to kill the lawyer, "one last job."

Candace wasn't supposed to repeat any of this to her daughter or anyone else, but she told Holly everything. Living just a few doors from her mother, Holly had seen the mystery man and his truck, but she hadn't been allowed to meet him yet. "He's not ready," her mother had explained.

Holly had been after her mother to find out more about him, but by June that had proved to be a frustrating task. He never gave her a telephone number, but insisted that he page her, usually from telephone booths. They also had no idea where he lived. He said he had a mansion in Las Vegas and a place in Denver, but he never asked her mother to visit either one.

The women looked on the Internet to locate any William Neal living in Nevada and thought they had hit the jackpot when they discovered a man by that name with an address in Henderson, Nevada. They got his number from directory assistance and called. A man answered, but he wasn't Cody.

Then Holly caught Neal in a lie. She was out driving one night when she saw him at a bank of pay telephones. The problem was he'd told her mother that he was going to be out of town that weekend. After she told her mother, they decided to try to find out where he lived and look into what recourse Walters might have to get her money back.

Walters discovered a little more one night when she and Cody went out and he stopped at a convenience store to buy cigarettes. She used the opportunity to look in the glove box and found the title to the vehicle; it was registered to a woman named Rebecca Holberton. There wasn't enough time to read more before she saw her date returning.

Now Candace Walters was really conflicted. She cared for him. He seemed to identify with her dreams of owning a home and not having to worry so much about money. He said when his ship came in, she would be rewarded for her assistance to him. In the meantime, he showed her a good time; she'd never had so many roses or ridden in so many limousines. Maybe, she reasoned, there was a good reason for the secrecy and even the lies. Something to do with being a bounty hunter or even his connections to the mob, something he didn't want her involved in for her own safety. He'd warned her repeatedly that it would be dangerous for her to reveal what he told her to others.

She wasn't ready to give up on him. When he asked if she would approach her daughter, Holly, about a job for him, she agreed. He seemed ill a lot—his cough was worse—but needed to make some money as the legal battle was going on longer than expected. Of course that meant he finally had to meet Holly at her mother's apartment.

When Holly showed up that afternoon, her mother was nervous, reminding her that she couldn't let on that she knew much about Neal. Holly was prepared to find him a little standoffish because of all the secrecy; when they met, however, he shook her hand warmly and turned on the charm.

Holly had to concede that he talked a good game regarding the real-estate business. He even knew some of the terminology, such as LTV, or "loan to value." She was also touched by his story about fighting for custody of his daughter; he even brought out a photograph of the child as tears welled in his eyes. From her own experience, Holly knew how strong the bond between a parent and child could be.

A couple of days later, she had him meet her partner and, after conferring, they gave him the job as an independent contractor—he could use the office (her mother bought him a desk and a telephone line) and company resources and split his commission with them. He started like gangbusters; she heard him taking in a loan application before he'd officially even settled in. However, the enthusiasm didn't last long. Within two weeks, he was complaining about being too ill to work. He coughed a lot and she had to admit that he didn't look good. He seemed tired, wrung out.

The job was an afterthought when he called Candace Walters one day in late June to say that his funds, at last, were going to be available. She'd been after him about her money, and had confronted him about the truck title and the woman named, Rebecca Holberton. Maybe she should have a talk with Holberton and find out what was going on. Now, he said, that wouldn't be necessary. She was going to get her money, and he had another surprise or two for her. First they were going to fly to Las Vegas, make a party of it. Then not only was she going to get her money back, he was going to give her $100,000 for having been so cooperative, as well as keeping his secrets.

In the days that followed, the news just kept getting better. He told her one day that he'd just bought them both a one-way ticket to Las Vegas. Once there, they were going to be handed the keys to brand-new Toyota 4Runner trucks, one of which would be hers to keep and drive back to Colorado. What's more, she wasn't going to get $100,000, she was going to receive $2.5 million; there would be $1 million in cash when they got to Las Vegas, and the rest was going to be wired into her bank account. He even had her call her bank to ascertain how to go about transferring such a large amount. Every day there seemed to be some new addition until, finally, in addition to everything else, he'd decided to buy her a mansion in Las Vegas, just a few doors down from his own mansion.

Walters was overwhelmed, though she confided to her daughter that she only half believed him. Holly worried about the outlandish gifts, but there wasn't enough time to process what was happening. Her mother was certainly happier than she'd seen her in a long time, and Holly didn't want to rain on her mother's parade. The worst that could happen would be for him to disappoint her mom; then they'd go after him to get her money back.

In the meantime, Holly was busy getting ready for a business trip back to Missouri to start a new branch of her business. Coincidentally, or so it seemed, Cody announced that he and Candace would leave for Las Vegas on Friday, July 3, the day before Holly was due to leave. They would be returning Sunday.

As the day for Holly to leave approached, she and her mother took their walks in the foothills and talked about how their lives would be changed when they got back from their trips. It was still hard to believe that it was going to happen, but Neal kept acting as though everything was going according to plan. He'd told Candace to get rid of her wardrobe and sell her car as she wasn't going to need them.

Holly was surprised when her mother told her that she was going to sell her car. It was just a little Toyota sedan, but she'd worked so hard to pay it off and was so proud of the accomplishment.

On July 1, Holly decided to pay a surprise visit to her mother. She arrived to find Cody knocking at the front door. He gave her an extra warm hug when she walked up. He was in a great mood.

Unknown to Holly or her mother, the day before he'd driven to a building-supplies store and purchased a number of items, including a seven-

and-a-half-pound maul. Afterward, he had driven home and bashed in the skull of Rebecca Holberton.

Candace Walters was flustered to find her daughter and boyfriend on the same doorstep. She and Cody were supposed to go out that night to celebrate, but he was early and she hadn't had time to shower. He said that he had only stopped by to give her something he had in a box in his hands, but he wanted to do so in private. He and Candace excused themselves, and when they emerged a few minutes later, they embraced and kissed.

Holly was uneasy about the display of affection. She just didn't trust the guy. As he was leaving, he hugged her. "If I don't see you again," he said, "have a great weekend."

When he was gone, Candace dragged her daughter back to her bedroom, hardly able to contain her excitement. Cody had dropped off a photo album with pictures of his mansion in Las Vegas, as well as the one that would be hers—proof that what he said *was* the truth.

Holly couldn't believe her eyes. The houses were huge, bordered with palm trees, and both had swimming pools. They looked like the sort of homes that movie stars lived in. He'd also given her a $50 bill, half of $100 that "The Family" had sent him, symbolic of his new status; he'd given her half. "He said, half of what was his, was also mine," Walters explained.

On July 3, Holly stopped by her mother's again. Candace was a bundle of nerves; part of it was paranoia. Cody had warned her that if she talked about any of what was to happen, there might be dire consequences, and she'd told

Holly everything. She placed her purse in the closet "in case it's bugged" before she would talk that morning. She just couldn't believe that the day had come, her dreams would be answered beyond her wildest imagination. It wasn't the money, though she wasn't going to turn *that* down, but rahter what it represented—time. Time to slow down and smell the roses. Time to watch her daughter grow to womanhood; maybe there'd be a grandchild some day. At least she would no longer have to worry about how to pay the utility bill or buy groceries and still make the mortgage. And she owed it all to Cody. He really cared about her, enough that he bought her a home near his. They had been wrong to doubt him.

Walters was in a rush. She was supposed to take her car to a dealership. She asked Holly to take a photograph of her with the car, admitting she was "a little sad" that she was selling it.

Then it was time for Holly to go. They hugged, holding each other tight, and wished each other safe trips. "I love you," they said to each other, and parted.

Later that afternoon, Candace called her daughter to say she'd sold her car for $3,000. Now she was really nervous. Cody was on his way. For the last time, they told each other how much they loved each other. Then Candace was gone.

Neal drove Walters to the town house on West Chenango, saying he needed to stop for her first "surprise." He used the garage door opener to enter the garage and close the door behind him.

"The place is a mess," he apologized with a smile as he let her into the apartment.

The light of the dying sun could only feebly make it through the paper-covered windows. Neal had been honest. The place was a mess. There were unwashed dishes and the remains of meals on every open space, especially a table over near the sliding glass door leading to the back-yard. There was a footlocker and a circular saw on the floor, along with a variety of other construction materials. She didn't take any particular notice of the black object over against a wall and only partially covered with a carpet remnant.

Neal led her over to a kitchen chair in the middle of the living-room floor. He had her sit down, and with a flourish, he produced a brief-case. It was heavy, as though filled with tens of thousands of dollars. He tried to place the blanket on her head, but she held up her hands.

"No, Cody," she complained. "I don't want to mess up my hair."

Neal shrugged and gently draped the blanket around her shoulders. "Well, promise to keep your eyes closed," he said as he walked behind her toward the closet where he kept the maul. He returned with the weapon partly raised, pausing for a moment to note how studious and trusting she seemed there in her white sundress.

The ax went up and then down again. This time he used the blade side of the maul to cleave deep into Candace's skull above her left ear. He yanked the blade out and struck again, near the first mark; as she fell, he struck her again on the neck. When he finished, he walked back to the closet and replaced the maul.

Returning to the body, he had one final act to

perform on Candace Walters, a woman who'd never done anything to harm him. A woman who'd loved him. A woman who'd given him her life savings to help him win custody of a daughter he'd never really cared about, except as a line of bullshit to win over the hearts of caring women. He unzipped his pants, pulled out his penis, and then urinated on his victim's head and shoulders.

A lot of blood was pooling on the floor, so he placed her head in a clear plastic bag. He didn't bother to wrap the rest of her in lawn bags, but dragged her body over next to the fireplace, where he covered her with a blanket.

That done, he dragged a mattress into the room near the sliding glass door so that anyone sitting in the death chair would be facing it. Holberton's body was off to one side of the mattress against the wall. He then screwed the four eyebolts he'd purchased into the plywood flooring at each corner of the mattress. Next he measured and cut four lengths of rope, one for each eyebolt.

He stepped back and surveyed his work. He was ready for the next phase of his plan. But first he needed to get showered and dressed. He was taking two young women out for a night on the town, and he planned on having a real good time.

Six

With a smile on his face, Neal asked Suzanne Scott to remove her glasses. When she complied, albeit reluctantly, he tied a piece of bath towel around her eyes as a blindfold. "Can you see?" he asked the twenty-one-year-old woman.

If she looked down, Scott could see the floor of the garage at her feet. She was getting nervous about where this dress rehearsal for her roommate's "surprise" was headed and decided that the blindfold attempt was good enough. "No," she answered, "I can't see."

Neal placed a strip of duct tape across her mouth. It was uncomfortable but not painful. Still, she wished he'd hurry and get his playacting over with.

She knew Neal through her roommate, Beth Weeks, a woman she'd met at work. Weeks was thirty-five years old, divorced with three kids, and struggling to make ends meet. They had became close friends and often went out together.

One of their hangouts after work, and sometimes even during lunch, was a dark, smoky bar called Shipwreck's. That was where she first saw and heard about a guy named Wild Bill Cody

Neal. Weeks and some of her other coworkers knew him from the bar, where he could often be found starting at noon until closing most any day of the week. He was a character who enjoyed playing the role of a cowboy. He was always in a black cowboy hat, black T-shirt, blue jeans, and if the weather was colder, he donned a black duster. But she had never actually talked to him until late 1997, about the same time she and Weeks became roommates.

Weeks wanted her to double-date with Weeks's boyfriend, Jimmy Gerloff, and Neal. Scott wasn't real thrilled about the idea; Neal was quite a bit older and a little strange, but with a lot of persuading, she at last agreed to go.

Neal called and asked her to meet him at the Sheraton Hotel at Sixth and Union. She was to let the front desk know that she was with him and his party. "They'll take good care of you," he said in that low, rumbling voice of his.

Weeks and Gerloff were already there when she arrived, but Neal didn't join them right away. Still, Scott had to admit that the guy seemed to have some pull. Everyone on the hotel staff was very nice and accommodating, making sure she had whatever she wanted in drinks and food. He finally showed up and escorted them up to a floor in the hotel that he'd rented out for the evening's party. She quickly discovered the reason behind the staff's attentiveness as Neal tipped lavishly.

By early 1998, Weeks and Gerloff had split up, and Weeks began seeing more of Neal. Scott began to learn more about Neal, and how he seemed to relish cloaking himself in mystery. Some regulars at Shipwreck's said he was a bounty hunter; others hinted that he might have once been a hit man for the mob.

Neal never told the women exactly where he lived. He said he split a lot of his time between Denver and Las Vegas, where he apparently had a home. He even showed them photographs of a mansion, which he kept in a white three-ring binder with sheet protectors. But he said he wouldn't stay there until his little girl, whom he was trying to win custody of from her wicked mother, could stay there with him.

As far as Scott could tell, Neal seemed to have another girlfriend, a woman named Angela Fite. One night he called and asked Weeks and Scott to come see him and "Angie" down at a swank south Denver restaurant. "We'll have a drink to celebrate Scott's birthday," he insisted.

They only stayed for one drink, but Scott left with the impression that Neal and Fite were intimate. Still, after the meeting at the restaurant, Weeks and Neal seemed to be together all of the time. Weeks confided that she was really starting to care for him.

Scott had to admit that Neal could be a lot of fun and that she benefited from his largesse as Weeks's roommate. He liked going out in limousines and threw money around without a care in the world. He would never allow anyone else to pay when they went out, whether it was dinner or the extravagant tips he insisted on giving the restaurant staff.

A night or so before her birthday, shortly after meeting Fite, Scott was asleep in her room when she heard Neal and Weeks enter through the front door of the apartment. A few minutes later, Weeks knocked and walked into her room.

"Cody wants to know if he can come wish you a happy birthday," Weeks said.

"OK," Scott answered sleepily, wondering what this was all about.

Neal came in and began tossing dollar bills onto her bed, $100 in all. "We'll use some of this when we go out to celebrate your birthday," he said. The gesture surprised her. She didn't really think of him as being a close friend, but later, Weeks shrugged and said that it was just an example of Cody's generous nature.

Around mid-June, Neal started talking to Scott about having "a surprise" that he was planning to give Weeks. He'd talked often about helping Weeks with her financial situation before, saying he was thinking about buying her a new car or helping with some of her expenses. This was different, he said; this was going to be a big surprise.

When she brought up the conversation later with Weeks, her roommate happily confided that he'd told her that he was buying her a home. She wasn't sure whether that also meant he intended to live with her, though he'd said something about wanting to keep some of his things there.

Neal said he also wanted to help Scott out. He asked her to work for him in "his" mortgage-lending business. He was talking about a lot of money, a lot more than she was making at her present job, and it involved some travel between Las Vegas and Colorado, which sounded like it could be fun.

Still, Scott had a hard time believing him. It just seemed too good to be true. But he kept insisting that it was, and then said he wanted her

to go with him to Las Vegas. His lawyers, it
seemed, were insisting that they meet her before
she was offered the job. He said they would be
gone for two nights, but she balked; she didn't
tell him, but she wasn't comfortable with the idea
of spending that many nights in his company in
a city that she didn't know. He was Weeks's boyfriend, and it just didn't seem right. When she
said that she couldn't go for that long, he
changed his mind and said they could go for a
quick trip, overnight and be back the next afternoon.

Scott decided she could at least go to Las Vegas
and see if the offer was on the up-and-up. It was
settled then, he said he would pick her up Sunday evening, July 5, and they'd come back Monday. He said there was just one other thing. He
didn't want her to mention his offer to anybody,
including Weeks.

The last request seemed odd. Scott broke
down and told Weeks. Her roommate was puzzled that Neal hadn't said anything. "Do you
think he can be trusted?" Scott asked. They
talked about it for a little bit; then Weeks answered, "I don't think he'd ever do anything to
hurt one of us."

Two days before the trip, Friday, July 3, Weeks
called Scott at work and said that Neal had made
plans for the three of them to go out. She said
she thought he might be taking them up to Cen-
tral City, a former mining town in the mountains
west of Denver that had legalized gambling casi-
nos in 1991. "Get home as fast as you can after
work," she said, "and get ready to go out. He
says it's going to be a big night."

When Scott got home from work, Weeks was

already there. She showed off several new outfits that Neal had bought her that afternoon during one of his famous shopping sprees. Weeks handed Scott a skirt. "Cody wants you to wear this," she said. Caught up in Weeks's excitement, Scott accepted the skirt.

The night began as a mystery. Cody had given Weeks specific instructions. After they got ready to go, the women were to walk across the street to a pizza joint. He would meet them there. The women did as told and had been waiting about ten minutes when Neal showed up about 7:00 P.M. The odd thing was that they didn't see him pull into the parking lot. He just walked up. He explained that his truck had a flat; he was getting it fixed at the tire store down the block.

As though frustrated, Neal said they might as well order a pizza and eat while they were waiting. He ordered and then, to Scott's astonishment, dropped to one knee and proposed marriage to Weeks. Her roommate giggled and told him yes. He then presented her with what certainly looked like a diamond ring.

Scott was still trying to comprehend what had just happened, when Neal popped up again and said that he needed to run to a nearby liquor store. When he was gone, she turned to Weeks. "I didn't know you guys were *that* serious," she said.

Weeks laughed. "It was just a joke," she said. She looked at the ring and frowned; it certainly *looked* real. But no, it was just a joke, she concluded again.

A few minutes later, Neal was back with several small airline bottles of alcohol. He invited the women outside to celebrate his betrothal and royal "proposal" to Weeks. He was dressed in his omnipresent black cowboy hat, black duster, and cowboy boots, but he'd eschewed the usual black T-shirt for a western-style dress shirt with mother-of-pearl snap buttons.

Neal was in a grand mood indeed, laughing and carrying on, talking about what a great time they were going to have that night. Rebecca Holberton had been dead and wrapped in black plastic for more than three days. He'd split Candace Walters's head open only eight hours earlier. But he was full of life when a white stretch limousine pulled up. Neal explained that this was another joke; they weren't taking his truck tonight—they were going in Wild Bill Cody style.

With Neal directing, they first went to two bars—Fugglies, where he went in with the women for a drink, and Shipwreck's, where, without explaining why, he stayed outside. Then it was off for the night's biggest surprise. He was taking them to dinner at the Diamond Cabaret, a "gentleman's club"—a restaurant and lounge on one side and a topless dancing bar on the other.

They went in the restaurant side and were seated immediately. Neal ordered rum and Coke while the women ordered beer. He, of course, picked up the dinner tab and drinks. He paid in cash, of which he had plenty, having gone to an ATM machine with Walters's debit card and removed $400. He'd already taken nearly $1,000 out of Holberton's account.

After dinner the two women went into the bathroom. While there, a woman approached, asking for Scott by name. When she identified herself, the woman said, "Cody wants you to follow me." Going along, they were led into the topless dancing section of the club. Neal was already there, sitting in front of one of the small stages where the dancers performed. He directed them to two seats and paid two dancers to strip in front of his two dates.

They didn't stay long. When the dance was over, Neal said it was time to leave. He handed Weeks and Scott handfuls of dollar bills and instructed them to put the money on another stage where a woman was dancing. The dancer smiled at him as though they knew each other.

Back in the limo, Neal said they could choose the next bar. The women decided on The Stampede, the country-western bar that Neal had frequented since back in the days when he was married to Tate. At the bar, they were joined at their table by several younger men, all trying to figure out if one of the two women with Neal was available.

Wild Bill Cody was in his element, lecturing the younger bucks on how to behave like a proper gentleman. "Stand up when a lady comes back to sit down," he told them when Scott returned from the rest room.

"A lady shouldn't have to light her own cigarettes," he said another time when they didn't react quickly enough when Weeks brought one to her lips. He, of course, had his lighter ready.

Toward the end of the night, Weeks and one of the young men got into a drunken disagreement about some trivial matter until Neal stepped between them. "You need to be polite to this woman," he growled. Though bigger than Neal, the other man backed down.

They got home about 3:00 A.M., and Neal spent what remained of the night with Weeks. Scott didn't see him there in the morning, but he and Weeks and her roommate's youngest daughter were all at the apartment that afternoon when she left to spend the Fourth of July with other friends.

Scott was back at the apartment on Sunday, July 5, to get ready for her trip to Las Vegas with Neal. She dressed in conservative business attire—a peach blouse and navy blue slacks. She'd packed another business outfit for the following day.

Neal picked her up about 7:00 P.M. When she got in the car, he said they were running a little early and that he wanted to stop for a drink at Fugglies. In the bar, he told her that before they left for Las Vegas, he wanted to show her the big surprise he had for Weeks and he hoped she'd be willing to go through a "dress rehearsal" for the event. They went back out to his car and soon arrived at a brown town house on West Chenango Drive.

The garage had an automatic opener, which Neal activated so that he could pull in and then immediately shut the door. That's when he said he wanted to blindfold her and put duct tape across her mouth. "That's how I'm going to have Beth do it," he explained.

Scott didn't want to do what he asked, but she assumed that the town house was the surprise that Beth had hoped for—a home of her own— so she went along with it for her friend. After blindfolding and muffling her, Neal had her take his arm as he led her through the garage and up the steps into the townhome. Inside, he picked up his cat, which he introduced to Scott, having her pet the feline's fur. He then led her down a hallway. Something was wrong. For one thing, there was no carpeting in the hallways, just bare plywood. She surmised that perhaps the home was being remodeled and the project was not quite complete.

Guiding her across the room, Neal brought her to a point where he told her to turn around and sit down. The seat was farther down than she had figured and she quickly realized that she was sitting on a mattress. He told her to lie back. She didn't want to, but now she was becoming afraid. She did as told but began to cry when he grabbed her wrists and then her ankles and tied each at a corner of the bed. She was spread-eagled, blindfolded, and badly frightened.

Neal seemed to have changed. Gone was the warm, friendly guy who was going to get her a great job and buy her roommate a new home. He told her to shut up and quit crying. "You haven't seen me get cold and mean," he warned, "and you don't want to."

She felt him fumbling at the buttons of her blouse until he had it open. There was a shock when she felt cold steel against her chest as he slipped a knife beneath the front of her bra and cut it off with a single stroke. He used the knife to slice her pants off her body and then her underwear.

"Do you want to die?" he asked her, pulling off the duct tape.

"No," she cried from fear.

"Then do as you're told," he said. "Just stay calm and stop crying."

Scott did her best to control her tears. She thought that she was about to be raped, but Neal suddenly stopped what he was doing and asked her a question. "Have you ever seen a human skull?" he asked.

"No," she said, not wanting to, either. She heard him get up and cross the room. A minute later he was back, removing her blindfold. He clutched something in a piece of paper. Delicately, as though it might break, he pulled an object from the paper. It was a bloody piece of bone with hair still attached. "You see that?" he asked, and placed it on her bare belly.

Neal left the piece of skull on her stomach for a minute, watching her reaction, before picking it up and tossing it over onto a large object wrapped in black plastic that she could see to her left. He'd been crouching at her side, but now he stood and walked past a chair at the end of the mattress and over to the fireplace. By lifting her head, she could see that he was standing by another large object that was covered with a blanket. He reached beneath the blanket, and to her horror, he lifted a woman's leg up. He let it fall back to the floor with a thud.

Next he walked over to the object in black plastic. It was another body, he said, and gave it a hard kick. All the while, he studied her face, looking for something.

Scott was sure that she was going to die. Why else would he show her what he had done and then let her live?

Neal came back to sit at her side, placing duct tape over her mouth again. He fondled her breasts and groped at her legs. Again she thought it was the prelude to rape, but he stood and said that he had to leave to get someone else.

"You better not make a sound," he warned.

He had colleagues upstairs who would remain there so long as she was quiet. "If they come down, they won't be as nice to you as me." He said they'd rape and then kill her.

Neal covered her from head to toe with a blanket. Then he left her there in the dark, thinking of the horror that surrounded her, and believing that he was telling the truth about "the others" upstairs. She concentrated on the country-music station that he'd left on the television for her entertainment, counting two music videos and two commercial breaks before she heard the garage door opening again.

Seven

July 5, 1998

All Angela Fite wanted when she entered the town house with William "Cody" Neal that night was a place to call her own. A home for herself where she could raise her two children in safety. A sanctuary. At twenty-eight years old, she also would have liked a man in her life who would treat her well, but she hadn't had much luck when it came to matters of the heart.

Back in 1989, Angela was working as a waitress at a restaurant when she met Matt Rankin and fell in love. He was big and tough, and handsome, too. She told her mother, Betty, that he reminded her of her father, Wayne Fite. Angela's dad was an ex-marine who served in combat in Vietnam and afterward worked in various, often mysterious jobs for the U.S. government. He and her mother had been divorced since Angela was five. She had lived with him for a couple of her high school years, but it was clear that she had missed him being in her life. Later, when looking for reasons for what happened, her mother would wonder if Angela stayed with Matt because of the resemblance and if when that resemblance proved to be a sham, she turned to Neal.

Both men were domineering, but there was at least one major difference: Wayne Fite loved his daughter dearly and would have never hurt her, but Rankin was abusive to Angela and would be arrested for it several times. About a week after she started seeing Rankin, Angela's younger sister, Tara, and Tara's boyfriend, Jeb, were visiting when they noticed a hole in the wall near the floor. "How'd that happen?" Tara asked.

"Matt kicked it," Angela responded with a shrug. "He was upset."

Later, as they left the apartment, Jeb told Tara, "That's the sign of a violent man. I don't see that relationship lasting."

The violence troubled Tara and later her mother, Betty, when she learned. It was not what she had hoped for her eldest daughter. When she was born, January 11, 1970, Angela had been a beautiful baby with a full head of dark hair, blue eyes, and rosy cheeks. She'd carried an easy disposition into childhood and adolescence, a straight-A student who never got into any trouble. She did have one childhood quirk and that was she named all of her dolls "Kayla" and told her mother that someday she would name her own daughter as she had named her dolls.

She and her sister, Tara, who had come along three years later, were polar opposites in their personalities. Angela was easygoing; Tara could fly off the handle at the slightest provocation. Angela kept her room neat; Tara was a pack rat. Yet the girls were nearly inseparable as children. Angela, as her family and friends called her, mothered her little sister whenever allowed. Tara was afraid of the dark and often crawled into her sister's bed. There they would take turns quietly singing songs until they fell asleep.

Betty wanted them to be close; that way if anything happened to her, they would have each other. The mother and her two daughters made it a point never to walk out the door, or hang up the telephone, without saying, "I love you."

When Angela Fite was a junior in high school, she told her mom that she wanted to go live with her father in California. She had reached an age when she wanted to know her father better. She stayed with him when he moved to Texas. Soon Tara announced that she missed her sister and went to join her in Texas. At first, it was only supposed to be for the summer, but when she got back, she cried for four days straight until resolving to move.

Betty always hoped her daughters would find nice young men, find careers they enjoyed and, when ready, present her with grandchildren to love. She was happy to learn that Angie had met a nice young man who'd recently graduated from high school and was in the air force. She hoped the relationship would last; from what she'd heard, Angie could have looked a lot further and not found a man who treated her as well. But Angie was young and not ready to settle down.

After a year, Tara moved back to Colorado. This time it was Angela who followed three months later to be near her sister. Betty was glad to have both living close to her and proud that they had both grown into such beautiful, intelligent young women.

But life took a turn for the worse for her eldest daughter. Shortly after Angela Fite moved into an apartment with a friend, Stacey, the other girl was in a traffic accident that left her in a coma with severe brain damage. Angela went to her hospital bed nearly every day, hoping that her presence might help her friend regain consciousness. But the girl was gone and wouldn't be coming back.

Then the brother of the boy she was dating, another nice young man, committed suicide. The resulting difficulties in dealing with that ended their relationship. Betty tried to comfort her daughter by saying that God must have some reason, some plan, that humans couldn't understand for such tragedies. But that only incensed her daughter.

"God doesn't make these things happen," Angela retorted.

Unfortunately, Jeb's prediction for the relationship between Angela and Matt Rankin was wrong. It did last. And it was soon apparent that Rankin was indeed a violent man, one who didn't limit his assault to walls. He drank a lot, which brought out the worst in him, but Angela thought her love would bring him around.

After about six months, Angie and Rankin moved into another apartment. Then a few months after that, Tara got a call from her sister asking for help. Angela told her that she and Rankin had been in a fight the night before. A rather one-sided fight in which he beat her up and attempted to strangle her. In desperation, Angela had jumped off the second-story balcony of her apartment to escape. He threw her stereo off the balcony after her.

The police arrived, and Rankin was carted off to jail. "I need you to help me move," Angela said to her sister. "I'm afraid he's going to kill me. . . . I could see it in his eyes."

"You need to leave him," Tara agreed. Her sister was always smiling, always upbeat, but now she was clearly frightened.

Tara and Jeb went over to Angela's to help her move. They were accompanied by a police officer, in case Rankin got out of jail and showed up.

Angela Fite moved in with her mother, who had remarried, to a man named Rod Von Tersch. Two weeks later, Angela was back with Rankin, assuring everyone that he'd apologized and seen the error of his ways.

Angela was already caught in the cycle that is known all too well to those who deal with domestic violence. There would be a period of remorse on Rankin's part: phone calls, flowers, and tearful contrition. Then something would set him off—generally right after he'd been on a binge or carousing for several days with other women—and she'd get beaten up. The police would show up, arrest Rankin, and Angela would swear it was over. Several times she moved out and in with her mother or sister. Then Rankin would show up, begging her to take him back, and she'd go.

"I love him," she'd explain to her family. They would have to watch her go back to wait for the next explosion, hoping he wouldn't put her in the hospital the next time. Or worse.

There were minor deviations to the cycle. For instance, Rankin learned that if he called the police first and came up with some story about how she'd attacked him, it would be Angela who was hauled off to jail.

Tara believed that her sister probably did hit

Rankin on occasion, but out of self-protection. It didn't give him the right to beat her up; he was a lot bigger than Angela was—the sort of hot-head who went to bars to pick fights. She was exasperated; her sister had been so strong in the past, so self-confident, but now she acted so dependent on a man who abused her. Tara grew more frustrated when her sister announced that she was pregnant. "How can you think of having a baby with him?" she demanded.

Angela replied that she thought having a baby would make the relationship stronger. But even after Kyle was born in June 1993, the violence continued. Only now, there was a child stuck in the middle, a child who often ended up in the care of Tara or her mother while Rankin and Angela dealt with their troubles.

Money was always tight. Rankin worked construction, which was seasonal, and Angela worked as a waitress. Still, she'd always impressed her sister and mother by how she could do with so little and still make whatever tiny apartment she was living in feel so warm and inviting. She loved her children; every little event in their lives—a first tooth lost, birthdays, holidays—a major event.

Angela might have looked at her family from two blackened eyes, but she was always smiling, even with a split lip, and confident that someday things would get better. She worked to make it so by studying at night, with Kyle cooing and playing by her side, to become a dental assistant.

Yet her life with Rankin was not getting better, it was getting worse. In the beginning, the violent episodes occurred maybe twice a year. Then it was every few months until by 1997 it was every couple of weeks.

"That's not love. That's not respect," Tara would yell at her sister. She begged her, "Leave him before you get killed." Angela just pointed out that she couldn't afford to live on her own and support a child, nor could she live with her mother or sister forever. She was sure that Rankin loved her; he just had some issues to work out.

After one beating, Angela Fite had moved back in with her mother when Tara came over and persuaded her to go for a bike ride. They had reached the top of a hill when Angela began vomiting. It turned out that she was pregnant again, and soon afterward she moved back in with Rankin. In April 1996, she gave birth to a girl, whom she named Kayla.

Again she hoped a child would save her relationship. But not one child or two changed Rankin, and it affected Angela more than just physically or emotionally. She would find work as a dental assistant, but her home life would soon interfere—whether it was a beating that she'd suffered or a court date that she had to make— and she would lose her job. Once at an office party, Rankin assaulted the dentist who employed her, costing her another position.

At last in January 1998, Angela's sister and mother persuaded her to leave Rankin and move into an apartment on the west side of the metro Denver area, closer to where they lived. She got a job at a bar called Fugglies, a small dive of a neighborhood bar.

Rankin hadn't been home for seven days when she moved out. When he finally came looking for her, he was upset that not only had she left him, she'd taken a job. He took her keys and purse and flung them into a nearby lake. He drove away in her van with both kids.

Not long afterward, Angela told her mother and sister about a new friend she'd met at the bar named Jimmy Gerloff. When she met Gerloff, Tara wondered what her sister was doing wasting her time on him. He was a fat, older man with a beard, who looked like he couldn't walk two blocks without having to sit down, and he was rude besides. Angela insisted that they were "just friends" and that he was helping her get to work since Rankin had disappeared with her van.

Gerloff also took Angela to the county courthouse to get a restraining order against Rankin. The order required him to return the van, the keys, and the kids. He gave back a set of keys and the kids, but left without saying anything about the van. Angela's family soon learned what kind of friend Gerloff was when she told them about the night he made a pass at her. They were driving in a remote area in his truck when he suggested that they become something more than friends. Angela rejected the advance and the next thing she knew, she was standing in the dark on a deserted road, watching him drive away.

One night, Angela called Tara and asked her to come over right away "to take me to the store." Tara drove to her sister's apartment with a girlfriend only to find Gerloff sitting at the kitchen table, reading the newspaper. He barely acknowledged Tara's presence, except through a cold, sideways glance that told her he didn't appreciate her being there.

Tara ignored him, but Angela made no move

as if to leave. "I thought we were going to the store?" Tara asked, her voice rising. Angie didn't move.

Angry, Tara left. Angela later told her that she hadn't wanted to anger Gerloff, whose behavior was beginning to worry her. She'd called him that night on his cell phone because she needed a ride to the store. He said he was nearby and would come right over. The weird thing was that he showed up on her doorstep in less than a half minute . . . as if he'd been right outside all along. When she could do so in secrecy, she'd then called her sister, hoping he would leave, but she hadn't wanted to press the issue.

That was the last time Tara had seen Gerloff. He seemed to pretty much drop out of the picture after introducing Angela to a friend of his, a guy who, he said, was a bounty hunter who might be able to help her deal with Rankin. A guy named Cody Neal.

Angela Fite told her mother and sister that not only was Cody a bounty hunter, but he supposedly had connections to the mob; he told her that he'd once been a hit man. When her mother voiced her concern about her daughter associating with an alledged paid killer, even a retired one, Angela assured her that in the past, he "only went after bad guys." She warned her mother and sister that if they ever met Cody, they weren't to mention what she'd told them because she'd been sworn to secrecy.

One day, Angela's van mysteriously showed up in front of the Von Tersch apartment. The vehicle was a total wreck, its engine shot. It was assumed that Rankin had brought it back, but that was dispelled when he called asking Betty if she knew the van's location. It was missing, he said. Betty didn't tell him, but Angela had told her mother some days before that Gerloff had found the van in the garage of one of Rankin's friends. To her knowledge, they'd left it there, and she had no idea how it ended up at the Von Tersch home.

More disturbing than the appearance of the van was a small writing pad discovered next to one of the seats. Inside the pad were scrawled notes all pertaining to death. Betty asked the police to check out who may have owned the pad and, perhaps, brought the van back. "What's it going to take?" Betty asked the police when they didn't seem to be very interested. "Someone getting killed?"

In the meantime, Cody Neal seemed to be quite wealthy and showered Angela with presents. There were flowers and limousines and expensive dinners—he even paid the baby-sitters lavishly, $100 for the evening. He also gave Angela Fite a pager, which he'd paid in advance for a year, so that he could reach her whenever he needed. When her mother asked what she saw in him, Angela replied, "He's not as good-looking as Rankin, but he treats me so good."

He was also mysterious. He wouldn't say where he lived in Denver, but said he had a ranch in Montana and a mansion in Las Vegas. Apparently Cody wasn't his real name. Angela said she'd learned that when he took her to a lawyer friend of his to talk about making sure she had full legal custody of her children. While there, the receptionist had said something about him changing his name to Cody.

"What's his real name?" her mother asked.

"Bill Neal," Angela replied, but made her mother promise not to tell anybody.

Angela's family had to admit that the mystery man had a sensitive side. He'd told her that he had a daughter and was fighting a battle to win custody from the child's "evil" mother.

Kyle and Kayla had come down with the chicken pox in March and Cody Neal volunteered to baby-sit the kids while Angela went to work. He bought Kyle an expensive video game and Kayla a set of dolls with a dollhouse. He also liked to play "bear" with Kyle, letting the boy ride him around the house on his hands and knees as he growled and carried on.

When Betty and Tara had asked to meet him, however, Angela had told them that he wasn't ready. Her mother almost got to see him once, though, entirely by accident. In April, she'd driven Angela to a convenience store to get milk for her children. When they pulled up next to the passenger side of a black pickup, Angie tensed. "Mom, there's Cody," she said, indicating the man at the pay phone. "Don't look at him. Don't look." Betty couldn't see him because the truck was in the way. He got in and left while Angie was in the store.

There seemed to be a lot of strange occurrences around her daughter involving Neal or his friends. One Sunday, Rankin brought the children to Betty's house when his visitation was over. Betty took the kids over to her daughter's apartment and was in the parking lot when Jimmy Gerloff suddenly popped up out of nowhere. Hiding her surprise, Betty smiled and asked, "What are you doing here?"

Gerloff shrugged. He just happened to be passing by.

Whatever concerns Angela's family had about Neal and his friends, the majority of their attention was taken up by Tara's impending marriage. She and Jeb had decided in January to tie the knot; a date had been set for July 25.

On Mother's Day in May, the two sisters were visiting their mother when Angela's pager went off. It was Neal and she rushed to a telephone to call him back. She returned and said that he wanted her to meet him at the Fiddlesticks bar.

Tara was driving the both of them and told Angela that she would drop her off only on the condition that she got to meet Neal. Angela hesitated, but Tara cajoled. "Come on, let's go have a drink." Angela at last relented, but she told her sister that she would have to wait five minutes before following her into the bar.

"Bullshit!" Tara said.

"Then I guess you don't want to meet him," Angela retorted as they pulled into the bar's parking lot. "There's his car."

Tara fumed. "Get in there," she said, forgetting in her pique her resolve to take down the license plate number of the vehicle Neal was driving. She stewed for five minutes and then went into the bar.

Neal and Angela Fite were sitting in the farthest, darkest corner of the bar. Another woman was with them. Tara walked up to the table as Angela introduced her. The man, obviously, was Neal. The woman was introduced as Beth Weeks, a new friend Angela had met at Fugglies who sometimes gave her rides when she needed to go to the store for groceries.

As Tara approached, Neal immediately stood up and got her a chair, holding it for her like a gentleman until she was seated. Tara had to admit that he was dressed nicely, in a western sort of way. He was wearing a black cowboy hat, a black silk shirt, and tight-fitting blue jeans. She was surprised by how smooth and young his complexion appeared.

Then again, everything about him seemed slick and rehearsed. He played the part of the gentleman, jumping up every time one of the women got up for something, or lighting their cigarettes about as quickly as they could put them in their mouths.

Yet he wasn't always so animated. Except when acting the gallant, he sat with his arms folded on the table, his head bowed as Angela and the other woman did most of the talking. Occasionally, he peeked out from under the brim of his hat at Tara, as if judging her. She thought it was creepy.

Neal perked up some when the subject turned to Mother's Day. With a tear in his eyes, he talked about how close he'd been to his mother and how devastated he was when she died. A moment later, though, he surprised Tara by asking what she thought of Rankin.

"He's a jerk," Tara answered.

Neal looked up from under his hat. "I'm gonna kill him."

Nobody said anything and the conversation went on. But Tara was stunned. How stupid, she thought. She hoped that her sister wasn't really contemplating having Rankin killed. But she thought Neal was a real idiot to make that announcement; he didn't know her. She figured he was just a braggart.

After a little while, Weeks got up to leave. Neal stood and escorted her outside. He'd been gone for twenty minutes when Tara asked Angela if she didn't think it had been a bit too long a good-bye.

"Oh, they're just good friends," Angela replied. She said that he was helping Weeks get custody of her kids, just like he was helping her.

"What if they're kissing?" Tara teased. But her sister insisted again that Weeks and Neal were just friends. Tara dropped the subject.

After Neal returned, the two sisters stayed only a few minutes longer. Angela wanted to get back to her apartment; she was going to cook dinner for him that night and needed to start preparing the food. He stood up with them but remained at the table, saying he'd be at Angela's in an hour.

Tara took her sister back to her apartment and waited with her, hoping to learn a little more about Neal. But when an hour passed, and then another without him showing, she left. She was unimpressed by Neal. She thought he had beady, sneaky eyes and a big mouth. She dismissed his claims to have been a bounty hunter or a hit man for the Mafia. Hell, her sister had broader shoulders than he did and could probably kick his ass.

"That guy is fuckin' weird," Tara later told Jeb. "I wanted to get his license number, but I forgot. . . . What gets me is that Angela believes all this crap."

The next time she saw Angie, she let her know what she thought of her boyfriend. "He's not good enough for you," she said. "He's old. Find someone who can keep up with you."

Angela always responded that Cody treated her well, which was more than she could say for Rankin, however much younger and better-looking he was than Cody.

Nobody wanted her to stay with Rankin. Her mother and sister had urged her to leave him before he really hurt her. She'd even had a falling-out with her father when she wouldn't get him out of her life. However, dating Neal seemed to be trading one problem for another.

About a week after meeting him at the bar, Tara called her mother from the gym where she worked out. Neal had followed her to the gym, she said. "He's out in the parking lot."

Betty was confused. Angela had told her that Neal was going to be in Las Vegas that weekend. Why the lie? Why had he followed Tara?

Tara decided not to tell her sister about the incident. However, Betty told Angie, who was bewildered. He wasn't supposed to be in town. But she didn't say much; whatever she was thinking she kept to herself.

As more time passed, Betty began to notice that Neal's stories—like the time he was supposed to be in Vegas but followed Tara instead—didn't always jibe. He was supposedly single, but he would only see Angie on weekends. Betty asked her daughter if she'd considered whether he was married.

"You think so?" Angela replied in a way that made her mother think that her daughter had been thinking along the same lines. She was concerned enough that she asked him. She happily reported back to her mother that no, he was not married. What's more, he had told her that he was going to buy her a home near where her mother lived. She wasn't supposed to tell anyone and again she swore her mother to secrecy.

Her mother thought it was just too incredible. "No man just buys a woman a house," she said. Angela had no real answer. Cody had told her that he had everything under control and not to worry.

Betty and Tara were too distracted by the upcoming wedding to give it much more thought. On June 13, her mother and sister and bridesmaids gathered for a bridal shower. Angela seemed to be in a particularly great mood. "Mom thinks I'm the prettiest one," she teased her sister.

In the middle of the shower, Angela was paged by Neal. This time when she talked to him, she was a little miffed. She'd received a bill from the lawyer, and Neal had told her that he would take care of it. He assured her that she didn't have to worry about the bill. He would make it up to her by taking her out to dinner that evening; he even sent a limousine to pick her up.

Strange things continued to happen to Angela Fite. She returned home one evening after work to find that someone had gotten into her apartment by climbing in a second-story window. Or maybe two someones. There was an empty soda pop can outside her front door and another inside. Stranger still, someone had neatly arranged her shoes in the closet by the front door.

Her first thought was that the intruder had been Rankin. The soda pop was an unusual brand his mother was known to buy. However, on second thought, he was not the sort to take the time to straighten her shoes. She wondered if there was a second intruder and if his name was Cody.

By the end of June, Angela seemed to have made a decision about Neal. The Fourth of July was going to be on a Saturday. Rankin was taking Kyle and Kayla to a lake for the weekend, so Angela brought them by her mother's house on Wednesday, July 1, for an early celebration. As the kids and their grandmother shot fireworks off in the street, the two sisters talked in the bathroom.

Tara took in Angela's thick dark hair, stunning blue eyes, rosy cheeks, and a smile that could make her day better just by seeing it. "Angie, you're so pretty," Tara said, "what are you doing with that guy?" She thought he was full of bullshit and said so. The hit man, the bounty hunter, the home he was going to buy Angela—just a bunch of stories to make him look like a big man.

Angela nodded. "I'm getting close," she said.

"What do you mean?" Tara asked, delighted.

"I can't say, but I'm almost there." Angela wouldn't go any further, but did say that she hadn't spoken to him for nearly three weeks. Not since just after the bridal shower.

But getting away from Neal proved harder than just saying she would. On Thursday, July 2, Angela was supposed to go over to Tara's house to help her clean in preparation for the arrival of her wedding guests. Her sister had offered $100 for the help and she'd readily agreed. However, that afternoon Angela called her sister and said that Rankin had not arrived yet to pick up the kids for the weekend. At 7:00 P.M., she called again. Rankin had finally picked up the kids, but now she was too upset to clean and was going out instead. "I'll come over tomorrow," she assured her sister.

Friday came and went without Angela showing up or calling until late that night. She said she was sorry, but something had come up again.

Angry, Tara said to forget it. "You know what," she yelled into the receiver, "I can't count on you. Every time I ask you for something, you let me down."

Trying to mend fences, Angela asked Tara if she was going over to their mother's for the Fourth of July. Tara replied cooly that she and Jeb had other plans. The conversation ended with Angela promising to drop by on Sunday morning, July 5, to help clean.

On the Fourth of July at her mother's house, Angela Fite was all smiles despite her sister's absence. She told her mother that on Monday, Cody was going to show her "a surprise" that he had for her. She was pretty sure that it was the house he'd promised; he'd even hinted that the remodeling was finished except for laying the carpet.

Betty had her misgivings. When something sounded too good to be true, it probably was. But Angela was happier than she had seen her in years, and she didn't want to dampen her spirits. If Cody was going to disappoint her, then she would have to deal with that later. In the meantime, what harm was there in dreaming?

Still, Betty could not shake a feeling that something bad was going to happen. A week or two earlier, there had been a report on the radio about two bodies being found in the mountains west of Denver. For some reason, she had suddenly thought of Angela and called her at work. She had been relieved when her daughter picked up the telephone.

Angela had laughed when her mother told her why she'd called. "Oh, Mom, you worry too much," Angela had said.

After the fireworks, Angela prepared to leave, hugging her mother. "I love you, Mom," she said.

"I love you, honey," her mother replied. "Be careful going home."

Sunday morning came and went, and again Angela was a no-show at Tara's apartment. Finally, early that afternoon, she called. She apologized, but Cody had decided to move up the surprise to that evening, and she wasn't going to be able to help that day, either.

About 4:00 P.M., Rankin showed up at Tara's apartment with Kyle and Kayla in tow. He said he'd gone by Angela's apartment to drop off the kids, but she wasn't home.

Tara paged Angela, who threw a fit when she heard that Rankin had tried to drop off her children. He was an hour early, she complained. She was still trying to run errands and get home in time to take the kids to a sitter so she could meet Cody for her surprise.

The outburst was unlike Angie. She was always so calm, so cheerful, even when her life was in shambles or she'd received her latest beating or disappointment from Rankin. Now she sounded hysterical, on the verge of tears. But she said she'd go home to wait for the kids.

A little later, Tara called her mother and told her about Angela's outburst. "Something's not right," Tara said. "You need to call her."

Betty tried to call and page her oldest daughter. But it was already too late.

When Angela Fite spoke to her sister, she was having a drink with Neal at The Bonfire Lounge. The bar was another of his favorite haunts, so he was well known to bartenders Maggie Champion and Ashleigh Raymondi. That evening Raymondi was off duty and had only come in to pick up a telephone number when she saw her friend Angie. She waved when Angie looked up for a moment from a rapt conversation with Neal. When he stepped away for a moment, Raymondi got a chance to talk to her privately.

Angie was excited. "He's going to show me something tonight. I think it's my new house. I think it's all furnished and everything."

Raymondi didn't think much of Neal. He seemed to have a lot of money, but she didn't consider him very good-looking and worse, thought he was just a con artist. Still, something else was nagging at her, something she couldn't define, when she told Angie not to go out with Neal that night.

Angie just smiled. "You're being overly protective," she said.

That night Angela Fite dropped Kyle and Kayla off at the baby-sitter's at about 8:00 P.M. The baby-sitter thought Angie was out of sorts, almost desperate to get going.

Angela drove to Fiddlesticks to meet Neal. He wasn't there, so she ordered a drink and waited. When he did arrive, he didn't come in but paged her from his truck and told her to meet him outside. They dropped her car off at her apartment and then drove to the town house on West Chenango where, he said, her surprise awaited.

True to his word, the town house was near her mother's house; in fact, the two residences were within view of each other. Neal blindfolded Angela to take her into the town house through the garage. He'd told her that the home was ready except for the carpeting so she wasn't alarmed when they crossed the bare wood floor.

After Angela was seated, Neal duct-taped her arms and legs to the arms and legs of the chair. He asked if she could get out. She tore through the duct tape, so he wrapped more tape around her arms and legs. This time she couldn't free herself.

When Neal was sure that she couldn't escape, he asked, "So how's your day going so far?" He didn't bother to wait for her reply but removed the blindfold. The room she sat in was filthy, the table and floor cluttered with dishes and the remains of old meals. An ashtray on the table overflowed with cigarette butts. To her right, there was a large lump beneath a blanket; a little farther, another lump wrapped in black plastic looked like a mummy. On the ground in front of her was a mattress. Large eyebolts had been screwed into the floor at the corners; ropes ran from the eyebolts beneath the blanket.

"Welcome to my mortuary," Neal said. He moved over to the mattress and pulled the blanket up to reveal the bottom half of a nude woman. He reached up her thigh and groped at her thighs until the woman beneath the blanket flinched. Then he lifted the rest of the blanket to reveal Suzanne Scott.

The eyes of the two women locked. "I'm

sorry," Fite said, "but we're not going to get out of here alive, are we?" Scott couldn't speak because of the duct tape over her mouth, but the fear in her eyes must have been answer enough.

Neal ignored the exchange between the women. Sitting down in a chair facing Angela, next to the table at the side of the mattress, he took out a pack of cigarettes and began to smoke. After a moment, he stood and allowed the two women to have a draw from his cigarette, pulling the duct tape from Scott's mouth so that she could participate. Whatever he was up to, he seemed to be in no hurry.

After a minute, he asked Fite if she wanted her own cigarette. "Yes, please," she answered.

"Can you smoke it without using your hands?" he asked.

"Yes, thanks."

Neal lit another cigarette and placed it in Fite's mouth. He didn't offer Scott one but instead retaped her mouth, this time much tighter than he had before. Suddenly he stood up. "I'm gonna go get a treat for my cat," he said, walking off behind Fite, toward the kitchen.

A few moments later, Suzanne Scott saw him reappear behind Angela Fite. He had the splitting maul in his hands, still covered with the gore from his previous victims. Before she could warn Angela, Neal lifted the maul above his head and brought it crashing down on the other woman's head. She fell to the side but was held to the chair by the duct tape as he struck again and again, like a man chopping at firewood.

Neal had hit Fite several times and was still going at it before Scott could turn her terrified eyes from the gruesome scene. Then, as if he'd finished some chore, Neal turned and calmly walked away.

When Neal returned, he didn't have the maul with him. Next to Fite's body, he stooped to pick something up. With the first blow, the cigarette Fite was smoking had popped from her mouth and onto the floor. He retrieved it now and settled into the chair next to the mattress to finish smoking it.

Suzanne Scott could hear Fite's blood striking the wood floor . . . not one drop at a time but like water pouring from a pan. Neal got up and placed a blanket over and under his victim's head. "So you don't have to listen to that," he said to Scott, and retook his seat.

Angela had been saying things she wasn't supposed to talk about, he explained. He regretted that it had been necessary, but he had done what he had to do.

"You see how calm and smooth I am," he boasted, taking a drag on his cigarette. "Bet you didn't know that was comin'."

Eight

After he finished Angela Fite's cigarette and watched television for a bit, Cody Neal stood and undressed. He left his shirt on but removed his pants, underwear, and boots. He came over to the bed and untied one of Scott's hands. Lying down next to her, he demanded that she manually stimulate his penis.

When he tired of that, he untied her other hand and her feet. Pointing a small-caliber handgun at Scott, he went and stood just behind the lifeless body in the chair. His victim was slumped over to her right at a nearly ninety-degree angle but was still held into the chair by the duct tape. He ordered Scott to kneel next to Fite and then to take his penis into her mouth.

Neal held the gun to her head. "Am I going to die?" she asked, crying.

"Do you want to die?" he replied.

"No." She could feel the hard steel against her temple. Her face was just inches from the body of the dead woman in the chair, but she did as she was told.

Neal ordered her back to the mattress. "Get on your hands and knees," he ordered. Then he finished raping her.

When he was done, he tied her up again. This

time he bound her legs together, tied to an eyebolt, but he tied just one of her wrists to the
floor; the other hand he left free. He sat down
in a chair next to the mattress and began watching the television. "Know what movie this is?" he
asked after a few minutes.

"No," she replied. She couldn't see the television well and didn't really care. She was thinking,
trying to do whatever it took to stay alive.

"Portrait of a Serial Killer," he said nonchalantly.

Twice as he sat there, sudden loud noises came
from what seemed to Scott to be the upstairs.
The second time, Neal got up with his gun and
went to check. He came back and told her it was
"the others" he'd warned her about.

As he sat watching the television, chain-smok-
ing, Neal talked to Scott, rationalizing his actions. His first two victims had betrayed him, he
said. They'd had fair warning. He'd hated to do
it, but Angela had to die because she couldn't
be trusted with his secrets.

Scott thought quickly. She had to keep him
from thinking that she couldn't be trusted,
either. "You're right," she said. "Angie couldn't
be trusted. You had to kill her."

Neal looked at her and smiled. She ventured
a request. "I'm a little cold," she said. "Could I
have a blanket?" She wasn't really cold, but being
naked made her feel even more vulnerable. Her
tormentor did as she asked, and she felt better.
It helped her keep her nerve in a room just a
few feet from three dead women.

"Why don't you come and sit next to me?"
she invited. The thought of Neal being close
filled her with revulsion and fear, but she wanted
him where she could see him all the time. She

didn't want him to sneak up on her like he had Angie.

Neal sat next to her. "Would you hold my hand?" she asked. She thought that if she held his hand, even if she fell asleep she would know if he tried to slip away to fetch his ax.

The only time that night they got up off the mattress was when she had to use the bathroom up the stairs. That in itself was a new terror. She'd never seen the "others," never heard a sound that positively indicated the presence of another living human being in the apartment—it was a town house, she reminded herself, the noises could have been the neighbors—but she'd heard something and Neal told her they might kill her. She had every reason to believe him. He warned her again when he escorted her to the bathroom, telling her not to look to her left as they went up the stairs. "The others are over there, and they don't want to be seen," he said.

Neal stood guard outside the bathroom door while she went in. After closing the door, she looked around and noticed something odd. The room was almost bare. There wasn't anything on the bathroom counter, like toothbrushes, soap, or a razor. There was a single bottle of shampoo and that was it. Odder still was a rope coming out of the wall next to the shower. The rope had a series of knots tied in it, but she couldn't understand what it was for . . . and didn't want to know. When she emerged, Neal was there to take her back down to the mattress, where he now tied just one wrist to an eyebolt.

The television stayed on all night. Or at least she thought it did, unsure if she had dozed off somewhere during that waking nightmare her

life had become. She kept expecting Angela Fite
to move, or maybe one of the other women. *This
isn't true,* she kept thinking. *This can't be true.*

In the morning, Neal untied her and let her
go to the bathroom and put on her clothes. As
soon as she was ready, they left the town house.
She looked back as they left, the scene forever
etched in her mind.

They got in the Toyota truck owned by Holberton. There was a brand-new pump twelve-
gauge shotgun behind the seat that he'd
purchased after the murder of Candace Walters;
he tucked the handgun into his waistband. He
drove to Scott's apartment, where he moved
quickly, picking up all the cordless telephones
and Scott's cellular phone, checking the bathroom to make sure there wasn't another in there.
Then he let her go in and shower.

"We still have a few places to go," he said.
"Don't unpack. I want it to look like we just got
back from our trip." Then he changed his mind
and told her to unpack. She opened her suitcase.
"Hey, you really packed well for the trip," he
remarked.

Neal told her it was time to go again. He hid
the gun under his shirt and again they went out
to the truck and drove off. He was hungry, so
they went to The Bonfire Lounge, where Maggie
Champion was bartending. He ordered himself
a Bacardi and Coke and Scott a beer; he also
insisted that they order something to eat, a
cheeseburger for himself, a plate of nachos for
her.

Champion thought the girl looked young and
asked for identification to verify her age. After
the food arrived, she noticed that her two cus-

tomers had barely touched their meals. "Food okay?" she asked.

"The food's great," Neal answered. "We just had a rough night." They left with their lunches unfinished.

The afternoon was spent shopping: cigarettes for the both of them, Tums for Neal's indigestion, and NyQuil for his cough. He drove to a mall and bought a tape recorder at Radio Shack, then on to a video store where he had Scott rent the movie *The Jackal*, a story about an international terrorist and assassin. He picked it out because her roommate, Beth Weeks, was always asking what he did for a living. "This will explain," he said of the movie. "Good enough for Beth."

At one point, Neal drove back by Holberton's town house. He said that they might have to go inside.

"Please," Scott begged. "Please don't make me go back in there." The image of Fite's feet and hands still taped to the chair would not leave her mind. She was afraid that if he took her inside, she wouldn't come back out alive.

Neal relented and they returned to Scott's apartment. They called Weeks at work and told her about "the trip to Las Vegas." "It was great," Scott said, conscious of the gun that Neal had on the table in front of him. "When you going to be home?"

That evening, after Weeks got home, they watched the movie. Neal acted like nothing was wrong. He joked; he teased; he was solicitous. When Weeks was gone for a moment, he promised Scott that as soon as the movie was over, the two of them would tell her what had happened.

After the movie, Neal led them to the kitchen table and told Scott to go ahead and describe what she'd seen. Scott began, but now that all the memories were there on the tip of her tongue, she couldn't. She began crying. Neal took over and told the story.

As he spoke, Weeks at first looked from his face to Scott's, which soon told her all that she needed to know about the veracity of what he was saying. She screamed. How could he have done such things? He responded by pointing the gun at her forehead and asking if she wanted to die. When she said no, Neal shrugged. He'd done what he had to do. If they wanted to survive, they had to do everything he said, exactly. Later that night, Monday, July 6, he got out his new tape recorder and, sitting at the kitchen table with the women, began making a rambling, nearly two-hour confession. As he spoke, he took the gun from his waistband and placed it on the table.

Scott and Weeks were forced to sit there and listen to him recount his reign of terror and murder, but at last Scott was allowed to go to her room and lie down. She shut the door and turned on her television, hoping to go to sleep. But sleep, if it came, was at best fitful . . . haunted. That morning she tried to stay in bed as long as possible so she wouldn't have to go out into the living room.

Incredibly, later that morning, Neal left the women alone while he went out. He threatened that they had better not call anybody or do anything because if somebody told the police or even if he got caught, more people were going to die. And that included them.

The horror of what he had already done and the threat were enough to cow them. They made no attempt to escape and get help. However, Scott gathered up all the clothes and anything else that she had with her at the town house the night before and put it all in a plastic bag. She stuffed the bag into her closet under other clothing. She told Weeks that if anything happened to her to give the bag to the police. Despite all that she had been through, she was thinking clearly enough to preserve evidence that could help convict her tormentor.

Otherwise, Scott and her roommate didn't talk much throughout that day. They just wandered around the apartment, feeling helpless. They had no doubt that Neal was sincere about his threats. He wouldn't hesitate to hurt them. Every way that they could think of to get help, they quickly decided wouldn't work well enough or fast enough.

Neal returned before they could come up with a plan. For the next several hours, he kept talking about leaving and committing suicide. He called Steve Grund, a television newscaster who'd been a drinking buddy. Grund wasn't in, so he left a message saying he had a "big story" for him and to call the number that he left.

In another twist, he told the women that they could summon a male friend over to the apartment if that would make them feel more comfortable. "Someone you trust, but who won't try nothin' with me," he said.

One name leaped to the minds of both women at the same time. David Cain. A thirty-four-year-old friend of Weeks's.

In contrast to William Lee "Cody" Neal's cowardice and indifference to life, there were a number of acts of bravery and selflessness by others during his rampage. Angela Fite's first response when she saw the spread-eagled and bound Scott on the bed was one of sympathy for the younger woman. Scott's courage and will to live may have been the difference that allowed her to survive her ordeal. Although rendered nearly helpless by fear and shock, Scott and Weeks didn't abandon each other when Neal left, nor did they take a chance that someone else might be killed in order to save themselves.

David Cain was another hero. Weeks called and invited him over without telling him of her predicament. He had no idea what he was stepping into when he arrived at the apartment and was confronted by a gun-bearing Cody Neal. He was told that it was his choice: stay with the women or leave. But if he left, Neal warned, there were going to be consequences for those he left behind. Cain looked in their faces and knew that the women needed him. He chose to stay.

They all sat down at the kitchen table again, and Neal played the tape that he made the night before so that Cain would know the full story. Close to midnight, Neal decided they were all going out . . . to the Allstars Strip Club. They stayed until closing, with Neal acting like they were all having a grand time, tipping the strippers lavishly, complaining that the drinks weren't strong enough. He insisted that his hostages drink with him and enjoy themselves.

The following morning, Wednesday, July 8, Neal began making plans for what was to happen next. He called Grund again and this time got through. At first the newscaster didn't believe his story; only after Neal put the women on the telephone did Grund realize the truth.

Neal warned that killing the three women might have only been the beginning. He was thinking of killing as many as thirty more people that he had in mind. When he got off the telephone with Grund, he told the others that he was at last ready to leave, find some lonely spot—maybe return to the scene of his murders—and kill himself. He'd decided to spare their lives, but only if they followed his explicit instructions on what each person was to do when he was gone.

Scott was to call 911 and tell the police what had happened. After she called, the three were to go outside and sit on the front lawn of the apartment complex. "I'm worried that if you stay in the apartment, Dave's gonna get hurt when the police come in," he said. "They may think he's the suspect. . . . I don't want him to get hurt." He continued with his instructions. When the police arrived, Weeks was to give them his pager number and a message regarding what time to call him. Then he was gone.

The plan fell apart after Scott called the police. She didn't want to sit on the front lawn. She thought it might be a trick, another "surprise" by Neal. He might see them outside and know that the police had been called; it could be a signal for him to return and shoot them on the lawn, so they stayed inside.

The police arrived quickly. Scott and Weeks were hysterical; Cain was on the telephone telling Grund what had happened since he spoke to Neal. It took the first officers on the scene a few minutes to make any sense of what they were hearing. When they did, they called the Jefferson County Sheriff's Office to say they'd just received a report of three homicide victims and another victim who'd witnessed the whole thing and had then been raped by an armed suspect who was still on the loose.

Nine

July 8, 1998

Even as Neal was giving his final orders to his captives, the bodies of the three murdered women were discovered.

When Rebecca Holberton didn't return to work on Monday, July 6, to start her new job, her supervisor thought she'd taken an extra day. When she didn't show up on Tuesday, her co-workers grew more concerned; it wasn't like her, except that they were aware she'd battled depression in the past. A friend from work decided to stop by the town house to check after work. She saw a vehicle in the driveway, but no one answered when she rang the bell.

When Holberton failed to show up for work on Wednesday, her supervisor at US West called her sister, Deb Lacomb, in Oregon. She had no idea where her sister might be. Holberton's co-workers called the Jefferson County Sheriff's Office and asked for an officer to check her town house.

Deputy Michael Burgess arrived at the West Chenango address about 1:30 in the afternoon for what he expected to be a routine "welfare check." Pulling up in his patrol car, he saw a man coming out of the town house next door to the address that he'd been sent to. "You know who lives here?" he asked.

The man shook his head. No, he said, the neighbors weren't particularly friendly.

He thought the apartment belonged to a blond woman. "A man lives there, too, sometimes."

Burgess went to the front door and rang the doorbell and knocked. Failing to get an answer, he went around to the side of the town house and climbed the locked fence into the backyard. A nine-year veteran of the sheriff's office, Burgess noted that all the windows on both levels, as well as the glass door, were covered with paper as though the owner was in the process of painting. The door was unlocked, so he opened it a crack and called out.

When there was no answer, he opened it a little farther and began to enter the half-dark room. He stopped short. He didn't know what had happened, but he knew that he didn't want to be there. Immediately in front of him was a table littered with the remains of all meals and cigarette butts, but it was the rest of the room that repelled him. It looked like a torture chamber. He backed away from the door and called in for help.

It had already been a busy day for Jefferson County chief deputy district attorney Mark Pautler. The office always had a chief deputy on call for major cases, and it was his turn. His first call of the day asked him to report to the scene of what was later determined to be a murder-suicide. As he was leaving his house, he called the sheriff's dispatch to check on the status of the search warrant so that he could enter the premises. The dispatcher asked, "Which one?" That's when he was told that there had been another apparent murder at a town house on West Chenango Drive.

Pautler first went to the murder-suicide with the search warrant. He then drove to West Chenango, where he talked over the situation with the investigators on the scene while they waited for another search warrant. He decided to see what he could by climbing the back fence and looking in through the sliding glass doors.

In more than twenty-five years as a prosecutor, Pautler had seen some grisly and disturbing crime scenes, but this one immediately jumped ahead of the others. A young woman sat in a chair facing the door, staring with sightless eyes. A blanket covered part of her, but he could see that she had been duct-taped to the chair. Her body was tilted at nearly a right angle, and there was a terrible-looking wound—or wounds, it was hard to tell—to her head. Blood was pooled on a blanket and on the floor. Strangely, there appeared to be a driver's license on her lap.

A mattress was on the floor with eyebolts at the corners, pieces of rope revealing the purpose of the setup. He could just see in the gloom what looked like another body by the fireplace; a white plastic bag had been put over the head, but he could tell it was filled with a dark liquid that he took to be blood. What looked like a third body was wrapped in plastic garbage bags by a wall.

So far, all that the police had was the name of one of the possible victims, Rebecca Holberton, who owned the property. Until the warrant arrived, they couldn't get close enough to read the driver's license. No one knew who the killer might be. Canvassing the neighborhood, the police had learned that a man lived at the apartment, but no one knew his name, his whereabouts, or much of anything about him.

Pautler and the others learned who the male occupant of the town house was when Grund contacted the sheriff's office. A few minutes later, they heard from Denver police who called in, saying they had three kidnap victims, one of whom claimed to have been raped and forced to watch a murder on West Chenango Drive by a man named Cody Neal.

The chief deputy district attorney left the walk-through of the scene to other deputy district attorneys, including Charles Tingle, who would be assigned lead prosecutor for the government, and the lead investigator for the sheriff's office, Jose Aceves. He drove to the Denver apartment where two of the hostages, a man and a woman, were talking to police. Suzanne Scott, the alleged sexual assault victim, was in a police car speaking with a detective.

Pautler spoke with the investigators and the two hostages, where he heard his first account of what Scott and the others had witnessed; he was told there was a tape-recorded confession. He also learned that Neal was armed with a handgun and, because shells had been found, was presumed to have a shotgun as well. The investigators were concerned enough about Neal returning to shoot the witnesses that they moved the interviews out of any potential line of fire.

It was early evening before the investigators were ready to page Neal and try to get him to give himself up. They didn't know much about him other than he was a cold-blooded and brutal killer who said he would kill again, and that he was capable of making "feeding the cat" jokes before murdering his third victim while a woman he planned to rape was forced to watch. They also knew by the manner in which he cooly planned and carried out his executions that he had thought through his actions for some time.

Neal returned the page from a cellular telephone and spoke first to his former girlfriend, Weeks, and then to Jefferson County sheriff investigator Cheryl Zimmerman. Neal talked to Zimmerman for about an hour while Pautler and other detectives listened to her side of the conversation and then looked over her shoulder at the notes she was taking of what Neal said in return.

The suspect was up and down: One minute he was the great killer, "scion" of a Mafia family; next he was calmly asking if he could have cigarettes and a private cell if he surrendered. Then he would be back claiming that he'd already murdered five hundred people and would kill again if provoked.

After about an hour, Neal asked to speak to a lawyer he knew. It so happened that Pautler knew that lawyer and was aware that the lawyer was no longer practicing law but was working instead as a sous-chef at a Denver restaurant.

When that information was relayed to Neal, he then asked for a public defender, but the investigators had several concerns about that request. First of all, they worried that they'd lose contact with Neal; he was on a cell phone, but nobody knew where he was, or if he had other hostages, or whether he was planning on more killing. There was also a possibility that the cell phone would cut out or lose power, and that if it did, Neal might not call back. The investigators were also worried that an attorney might tell him to quit talking, or might try to cut deals with them to get him to surrender.

The police were under no constitutional obligation to provide an attorney for Neal at that time. Contrary to television dramas, until placed in custody a suspect doesn't have the right to ask to have an attorney appointed for him, or for one to be present during an interview. Nor would Neal have the ability to later claim that he had not been warned of his Fifth Amendment right against self-incrimination, also because he was not in custody. On the contrary, Neal had spent a considerable amount of time and effort incriminating himself—first in front of Scott, then through subsequent confessions to his hostages and on a tape recording, and, finally, to Zimmerman.

In fact, until Neal was in custody, it would remain a police case, not under the direction of the Jefferson County District Attorney's Office. Pautler was there in an advisory role, but the police priority was to capture a confessed, and witnessed, mass murderer. There was every reason to believe him when he said that he had killed more than the three women who'd been found, and that he was capable of killing others. They knew that he was armed and dangerous. Decisions needed to be made and they needed to be made fast; nobody wanted him on the streets for a moment longer than was necessary.

A police officer could have posed as a public

defender and there would have been no reper-
cussions because the high courts have ruled that
the police may use lies and deceit in order to
apprehend someone who is a danger to the public. However, the concern in this case was that
Neal was obviously intelligent, at least in a "street
smart" sense, and they worried that he might trip
up a police officer with a legal question.

To buy time, Pautler wrote Zimmerman a note
saying to tell Neal that a public defender would
be available in twenty minutes. He then called
and talked to his boss, District Attorney Dave
Thomas, about posing as a public defender. Both
knew that his subterfuge would have repercus-
sions. A defense attorney would be sure to raise
the issue in some fashion—whether to appeal
Neal's case if he was convicted, or by bringing it
up to the Colorado Supreme Court's attorney re-
view commission as an ethics violation that could
jeopardize Pautler's standing as a lawyer.

Pautler believed that he could make legal arguments for the deception. One, as a deputy district attorney, he was a sworn peace officer with
the authority of a police officer, including the
ability to make arrests and conduct investiga-
tions. Two, he knew that the code of professional
conduct contained language that stated that the
rules governing attorney conduct—including
those prohibiting deception—were not hard and
fast, and that they seemed to indicate that lawyers
should use their common sense in unusual circumstances. There was no guarantee that the
courts would agree with either of his contentions.

Thomas believed that it was the best course of
action, but he left the decision to his chief deputy. With visions of the crime scene fresh in his

mind, Pautler decided that the public's safety outweighed the personal risk. He wrote Zimmerman another note, this one telling Neal that public defender "Mark Palmer" had arrived. He had decided to use a pseudonym in case he had ever had any dealings in the past with Neal or anyone he might have known.

Zimmerman handed Pautler the telephone. Avoiding any discussion of constitutional issues, such as Neal's rights, he told Neal that he was "looking at some pretty heavy stuff."

Neal's reply was all bravado. "I'm one of the most dangerous people you will ever have the chance to represent," he said. "This is not a game."

As the discussion with Neal went on, the Jefferson County SWAT team was gearing up to nab Neal when the moment came. That moment arrived late that night when, as he'd arranged with Pautler, Neal drove Holberton's truck into a parking lot of a department store.

Before he could move, the SWAT team swarmed over him and forced him to the pavement at gunpoint. A .25-caliber loaded handgun was found on the seat; a twelve-gauge shotgun was behind the seat with one shell in the chamber and two more in reserve. Boxes of ammunition for both weapons were also found on the seat, as were credit cards and other items belonging to Rebecca Holberton and Candace Walters.

Pautler was present at the arrest but did not attempt to talk to Neal. Nor did Neal ask to speak to Mark Palmer or any other lawyer when advised of his Miranda rights: that he could ask for an attorney to be present and that he had the right to remain silent.

"I understand," he said. But Wild Bill Cody Neal had no intention of keeping his mouth shut.

Ten

Holly Walters began to worry on Monday, July 6, when she didn't hear from her mother. She and her partner had left on Friday morning, July 3, for the twelve-hour drive to Missouri. She expected to be gone three weeks and took their time on the drive, arriving Saturday.

Sunday had been busy. Her partner's parents lived in Missouri and had an outing to the lake planned. Holly forgot her concerns about her mother and Cody in the fun, which turned to a disaster when the canoe that she was in with her dog and partner overturned in a lake. The dog received a cut and had to be taken to a veterinarian for stitches. By the time all the excitement died down that evening, Holly figured that her mother might have been too tired to call . . . or maybe delayed. But when the next morning passed into the evening, and she couldn't reach her mother, she knew something was very wrong. Even if she'd run into car trouble, or stayed another day or two, she would have made contact, she thought as she went to bed that night.

Holly Walters woke before dawn in a panic. She called her mother's apartment, tried her cell phone and pager. Nothing. "I'm going home," she told her partner, who insisted on coming.

They drove straight through, getting to Denver in the early evening.

Holly went straight to her mother's apartment, hoping to find that her mother was just so caught up in her new life as a millionaire that she hadn't gotten around to calling. But it was obvious that her mother hadn't been home since she left with Cody. Then she saw her mother's cell phone and pager on the table and realized that they must have been left behind. She searched the house and found cell and pager numbers for Cody. She tried both, but there was no answer. . . . She wondered if they'd been in an accident . . . but no, something told her that this was Cody's doing. The bounty hunter. The hit man. The con man.

She thought she had an idea where he lived, in some town house complex over on West Chenango Drive, so she armed herself with a hammer and a knife and went there to find her mother. She got there and looked in the windows, not knowing that she wasn't at the right address, though her mother's body and those of Rebecca Holberton and Angela Fite were nearby . . . beyond any rescue.

Holly Walters was out until after midnight before going home. There was no rest there, however. Only tears and fears. Finally, at 3:00 A.M. on Wednesday, July 8, she called the cellular number that she had for Cody and was surprised when a male voice answered. "Cody?" she asked.

"No," Neal started to respond, then recognizing her voice, said, "Oh, hi, Holly," and proceeded to feed her a story. They were in a little town about three hours from the Colorado border, but there'd been a little accident. Her mother, he said, had hit a deer, which had forced her off the road. She'd suffered minor injuries— a few scrapes and bruises—but otherwise she was fine. Five days after slaughtering Holly's mother, he even made a joke about her notoriously poor eyesight at night. She was back at the hotel, he said. "I was just out trying to get something to eat."

When he asked how her trip had gone, Holly told him about the boating accident. He responded by saying that he was just glad that everybody was OK.

"Yeah," she agreed. "When you get back to the hotel, have my mom call." Somewhat relieved by Neal's assurances, Holly lay down and soon fell asleep. She woke up after just a few hours, and knew that Cody was lying. *She would have called,* she thought as she got up. She was sure that Cody was somewhere in the Denver area.

Still, Holly Walters was hesitant to call the police. It would be admitting what she didn't want to even contemplate. She spent the day driving around, hoping to spot Neal. *Maybe she's a hostage or injured, but still alive.* At 10:00 P.M. she knew she had to file a missing persons report with the police. She called and gave the officer a description of her mother and of Cody Neal; she also gave the officer Neal's license plate number and Social Security number, which he'd supplied when applying for work at her company. The officer told her it might be twenty-four hours before her mother would actually be listed as a missing person.

Ten minutes later, the police called back. A detective told her that they might have some information about her mother, "but we need to send someone to talk to you."

"That does not sound good," Holly responded.

"Not good or bad, we just need to talk to you in person," the detective said.

Actually, it was nearly three hours before a detective arrived. When he did, he told Holly that they'd apprehended William "Cody" Neal that night and that there were three bodies in a town house.

"Is one of them my mother?" she asked, fearing the answer but needing to know.

"Yes," he said.

After the detective left, Holly Walters fought back her tears and called her father. The newspapers would be out in a few hours, and she didn't want him to learn the news that way. Then her grandmother called to see if she'd heard anything from Candace. Holly lied and said there'd been no word. She wanted the old woman to get her sleep, as she was going to have a tough day to deal with come morning. After she hung up, Holly let the tears come freely.

The family of Angela Fite had also been worrying for days. On Monday her mother, Betty Von Tersch, had tried to page and call her eldest daughter from work but got no answer. It worried her a little, but she thought Angie and Cody might have gone somewhere to celebrate her "surprise." Possibly even eloped without telling anyone.

Then she got an alarming telephone call. Angie hadn't picked up her children, Kyle and

Kayla, from the baby-sitter. Von Tersch couldn't believe that the baby-sitter had taken so long to contact anyone, but her mind quickly jumped to more important concerns. Where was Angie? She told the baby-sitter that she would be by directly to pick up the children. Then she called Angie's employer, who said she hadn't been in to work, nor had they heard from her.

Von Tersch left and decided to swing by Angie's apartment before getting the children. If something was wrong at the apartment, she didn't want the kids seeing it. The landlord didn't want to let her in the apartment. "You have to," she pleaded. "I have to know if she's dead or alive."

The landlord gave in. The windows were open, and Angie appeared to have been doing the laundry when she left, but she was not there, nor was there any sign of foul play.

Von Tersch left to pick up her grandchildren. After that, she wasn't sure what to do. *Maybe they went to Las Vegas and got married,* she thought. *Maybe her pager doesn't work there.* But Angie wouldn't have left her children with a baby-sitter without telling someone. She began to imagine all the horrible things that could have befallen the couple in Las Vegas; maybe something had gone wrong with Neal's mob connections. Without any other plan, she sat on her front doorstep, looking down the street, waiting for Angie to show up.

"Why is Mommy not home?" Kyle asked.

"I don't know, honey," she answered. "I don't know."

The sun came up on the next day, Wednesday, July 8, with still no word from Angie. About 1:00

P.M., Von Tersch decided to take the children to get haircuts. On the way, she passed West Chenango Drive, a block from her house, not knowing that her daughter's body was about to be discovered there by Deputy Burgess.

The more time passed, the more Von Tersch sensed the coming news. She called Matt Rankin and asked him to pick up the children. She felt that she was soon going to have to do something that would be easier if the children were not present.

Von Tersch was sitting out in front of her home when she saw a police car drive by at about 8:00 P.M. She told Rankin, who was in the basement with the kids, but he shrugged. It was not unusual for a police car to drive through a neighborhood. But Von Tersch knew that it was somehow connected to her daughter's disappearance. She went to bed but tossed and turned until about 5:00 A.M., when she got up and called the police to file a missing persons report. She tried to page Angie again, but there was no return call. She was getting ready to go to work when Tara called.

As usual, Tara had been awakened by the news on her clock radio. She was still sleepy and wasn't sure she heard right when the broadcaster said something about murders—two were dead in an apparent murder-suicide, and another two women were also dead . . . and something about a bounty hunter. A minute later, Rankin had called.

"You hear the news?" he asked. A couple of people were dead, including a bounty hunter.

The coincidence of her sister being missing, last seen in the company of an alleged bounty hunter, was too much. She called her mother and suggested that she call the police and try to learn more.

"Mom," Tara said, "he could be a serial killer, for all we know." Angie could have eloped with Cody, but she would have left the kids with Tara or their mother.

Betty Von Tersch turned on the television. The newscasters said that there'd been a multiple homicide on West Chenango Drive. She knew the town houses that they were talking about. . . . Heck, if she stood on her front porch, she could look right at the backyard of the town house in question. She couldn't seem to get through to anyone with the police who seemed to know anything, so she decided to go look for herself. She drove down to West Chenango, but the street was sealed off with yellow crime-scene tape. She could see a number of police and other official-looking cars parked down in front of the town house.

With dread seeping into her every thought, she flagged down a sheriff's patrol car that was leaving the scene. "I have to talk to you," she said. Her daughter, Angela Fite, was missing, last seen in the presence of a man named Cody. A bounty hunter.

"Where do you live?" the deputy asked.

Von Tersch told him and he said to go home and wait, an investigator would be sent to talk to her. The investigator arrived at the same time as Tara. The women asked if the news report was true—two women and a bounty hunter were dead. The investigator shook his head. No, three women were dead and a man had been arrested the night before for their murders. The coroner was trying to identify all the women, but he was not finished "unwrapping the bodies."

The investigators asked if they knew the alleged bounty hunter's real name. The women had been talking about him as Cody. Von Tersch remembered her conversation with her daughter. "Bill Neal," she said.

After the investigators left, saying they would get back to her shortly, Von Tersch was suddenly overwhelmed by the horror. Unwrapping the bodies? Had they been hacked to pieces and the remains placed in bags? This couldn't be happening. Tara had to calm her down. . . . It didn't mean that necessarily, she said.

With no more information, Von Tersch and Tara drove to Angie's apartment to fetch clothes for the children. When they arrived, they noticed a man sitting in a van, looking up at Angie's apartment. Tara figured that he had to be a cop and walked up to him. "That's my sister they're talking about on the news," she said. "What are you waiting for?" The detective replied that he was waiting for a search warrant; this was a murder investigation and he had to go by the book.

Von Tersch spent the rest of the day in a fog, and friends and family called with questions she didn't have answers to. Rumors and partial truths flew like birds. There was a news report saying that one of the women got away. They were talking about Suzanne Scott, but Von Tersch dared to hope that the survivor was her daughter. She kept waiting for Angie to call and say something like, "You'll never believe what happened, but I'm OK." There would be sadness for the other victims, but at least her daughter would still be alive.

Maybe they've got it all wrong, she thought. Maybe some other women had been murdered by some other bounty hunter. Angie and Cody would return from an elopement, puzzled by all the attention.

Then the coroner called and asked for a member of the family to come and identify Angela's body. Betty left that to her ex-husband, Wayne Fite, who'd come to town to marry a daughter off, not bury one, and to her current husband, Rod Von Tersch. The coroner had done his best to clean up the damage inflicted by Neal, but there was no denying that the woman lying on that cold steel table was Angie. She would not be coming home to her children and family ever again.

Even as the families of the murdered women were learning the horrible truth, so was the rest of the world. A media feeding frenzy ensued, some of it sparked by Neal's willingness to talk to reporters.

The day after his arrest, he told a television reporter, "I will state as fact there are two other bodies they haven't found yet that I know of." He wouldn't elaborate any further.

Neal denied being on drugs at the time of the murders. Also, there was a "common thread" between the three murder victims, he hinted. Then he apologized to the friends and families of the women and to his own family and friends. "I am truly sorry," he said, adding that he was worried about the effect his crimes would have on his young daughter.

He finished by publicly firing his attorney, public defender Jim Aber, a longtime opponent of the death penalty. Neal said that he wanted to plead guilty immediately, but Aber was trying to talk him out of it. "As of this moment, you are fired," Neal said into the television camera; he wanted another attorney.

The authorities responded to Neal's claim of other homicides. "We considered the possibility that there might be others, but at this point, we don't have direct evidence that there are," said sheriff's sergeant Jim Parr. "Nobody's unaccounted for.

"The more he would like to tell us, the more we're willing to listen. We're investigating everything we can think of involving Mr. Neal, all the way back to the date of his birth."

As the days passed and rumors were hunted down and discounted or embraced—at least for the time being—small details about the victims and their killer began to emerge in the press.

In one report, Holberton's ex-husband, Rodney, remembered her as filled with joy and warmth for others. "She always had a smile on her face. I mean, she was a kind, gentle person."

George Holberton said that he didn't understand how his former daughter-in-law could have been mixed up with someone like Neal. "Rebecca was this very gentle, kind of shy young woman, as I remember," he told the press. "Not the kind that would get involved with anyone shady. It would be beyond her to harm anyone else."

He recalled that she was "pretty conservative . . . didn't drink or smoke or even go out much with men." Even after their divorce eight years earlier, his son had remarked how she was the one woman he could trust. George noted that his daughter, Tammy, had remained Rebecca's best friend. She was "shocked and distraught" that the man she'd met in Las Vegas had murdered Rebecca.

In another story, Rebecca's neighbors told the media that she did not return greetings and kept to herself. After moving in, she'd even covered her windows with brown butcher paper, which had remained up for most of the two years that she lived in the home.

The press reported that Angela Fite's relationship with her estranged common-law husband, Matt Rankin, had been an abusive one and he'd been arrested for domestic violence. She'd left him and was working as a dental assistant when she met Neal, according to the reports.

A week after Neal's arrest, Angela's family held a press conference. It had seemed that in some ways, it was Angela and the other women who were being scrutinized, not Neal. If nothing else, they were represented as having been particularly gullible, or even unintelligent lonely hearts just waiting for something bad to happen.

"We would first like to express our gratitude for the tremendous support we have received since the death of our beloved Angie," said Deborah Hill, a family friend who read from a prepared statement.

Hill asked the public and press to remember that "Angie and the other victims were innocent of any wrongdoing. . . . Angie simply put her trust in the wrong person, as apparently did the other two victims, which resulted in this senseless tragedy."

The family, she added, was "distressed" to

have learned about her death from news reports. "Her name was released to the public before we were ever notified. No family should have to receive such horrific news through the media." She said that the family's priority would be helping Kyle and Kayla deal with the loss of their mother.

Candace Walters was recalled by family and friends as a small woman who enjoyed nature walks and lived for her daughter, Holly. "She was the most generous person I knew," her ex-husband was quoted as saying.

But what of Neal? Why had he suddenly "snapped" and murdered three innocent women? Holly Walters told the police that her mother had told her about a letter she'd penned and left with a friend, "just in case" something happened between her and Neal. The police had been unable to find the letter.

A report filled in some of the gaps in what Suzanne Scott and others were able to tell the police about his behavior and activities. In the morning after he left Scott and Beth Weeks in their apartment, too stunned to even try to seek help, he went back to The Bonfire Lounge and started drinking his usual Bacardi and Coke.

On-duty bartender Ashleigh Raymondi recalled that he'd bought the woman sitting next to him a drink and then asked her to change seats with him. "So I got a clear view of the doors," he said, indicating the front and back entrances into the bar.

"Why?" the woman had asked.

"I'm a bounty hunter," he'd replied. "I have to watch my back."

Bartender Maggie Champion, who'd served

Neal and Scott the day before, was in the bar that same morning, off duty and sipping coffee, when Neal asked her if the bar pay phone would "block out the number if I make a call." She assumed that for whatever reason he didn't want the number to show up on someone's Caller ID. "I don't know," she said with a shrug. She found it curious when she stepped outside later and saw him talking on a cell phone.

Neal spent most of the morning in the bar with a $50 bill and several other denominations spread out in front of him. When Raymondi moved to deduct one of his rounds from the fifty, he grabbed her arm and told her to take one of the other bills. The $50 bill, he said, was for a bartender at another lounge.

A little later, two women entered The Bonfire and sat about ten feet away from Neal. He pushed $20 at Raymondi and told her, "Give the ladies anything they want." The women accepted the drinks, but the strange thing was that he never looked up from beneath the brim of his black Stetson, or tried to talk to them, though they sat there for an hour.

Raymondi recalled talking to Angela Fite on the night she died. She said something about Neal taking her to a house that he was going to give her that night. "Something was tugging at me," the bartender recalled. "Something was telling me to get her away from him. Seeing the excitement in her eyes just kills me now. She was so happy, thinking this was her future with this guy. She's not the gold-digger type, but she was attracted to Cody. I don't know why."

Neal's main attraction was the way he tossed money around, Raymondi said. "He wasn't good-looking. He had no pizzazz. But he always told everyone he was worth millions." She noted that she warned Angie not to go out with Neal. "I was just going on a feeling about him," she said. "I just thought he was a liar, a total con artist. I didn't think he was going to kill anybody. I just thought that he was full of crap."

He did make a halfhearted attempt to pick up Raymondi that morning. "You'd be a lot of fun to go out with," she recalled him saying. "What are you doin' after work?"

Raymondi said that she shook her head and told him, "I don't date customers."

"Your loss," she said Neal replied with a shrug. He left her his usual extravagant tip and even threw $5 to a bartender who'd just come on duty and hadn't served him. "You'll never forget me," he said, and strolled out of the bar. Five minutes later, another regular came through the door with the news that Angela Fite was missing.

Neal had gone on to Shipwreck's, where he gave one of the female bartenders the $50 bill that he'd been saving. "I've tried to analyze that, over many sleepless nights," the woman told a newspaper columnist. "First I thought maybe it was so I wouldn't tell Angie I'd seen him with another girl on Sunday night. You think all kinds of things. Was it bribe money? A tip? Or did he want to kill me, too? All kinds of stupid things go through your head."

Raymondi might not have seen much in Neal, but others knew his appeal to women. "He was the gentleman's gentleman," said Louis Veraldi, a cook at one of Neal's hangouts and one of his few male friends. "I've never met a guy who's nicer, who treated women with more respect.

"It was almost like he was from medieval days. He'd open doors for men or women. He walked women to their cars to make sure no harm would come to them. And he was a very generous man."

Florist Beverly Wise recalled the polite man who bought roses for strippers. "I always got the impression that if you were on a date with Cody, you were queen for a night," she said.

Duane "Dog" Chapman, a big, strapping bona fide bounty hunter, told newspaper reporters that Neal had provided him with some tips that led to the capture of a few wanted methamphetamine users. The man he knew only as Cody would occasionally call up and volunteer his services. "But I never paid him for his information," Chapman said, "or, for that matter, never knew his real name."

It was as close as Neal had ever been to being a bounty hunter. As the press discovered, he'd occasionally worked as a house painter but had held no steady job for more than two years.

Meanwhile, Neal's family did their best to explain the unexplainable. Nephew D. J. Hardy, a Denver resident, acted as the family's spokesman, saying that Neal had changed following the death of his mother and subsequent divorce and loss of his business. "The last few years he has been to himself, pretty distant from the family," said Hardy. "I want to make it real clear that we still love him. But everybody is upset. They are really mad—mad at him for what he did. We hope justice will be served in this case. We are behind the families of the victims one hundred percent."

Eleven

As they began to piece together the events that led to the murders, the investigators wondered about the influence that Neal seemed to have over his victims. He was apparently able to juggle his time between them, keep his whereabouts a mystery, as well as his history. . . . Yet, he had gained their trust to the point that they were easy prey when he finally decided to murder them. He wasn't particularly attractive, but there was something about him that disguised the killer inside.

They began to learn more when they located his four ex-wives. They were all attractive, intelligent, independent, trusting women—from what they could tell, just like his victims. The first wife had not wanted to get involved, though she said she was not surprised by the violence and was afraid of him.

They learned much more from his second wife, Karen Wilson, who told them about the handsome young man she had met in her Washington, D.C., store. Like the first wife, she was afraid that Neal would somehow "beat the rap" and get out of jail. But she felt that she owed it to the victims to tell the police what she knew about the "real" William Lee Neal, a man with an explosive temper, beset by jealousies and imagined betrayals.

Wilson heard of the murders on July 10, her birthday, and she'd had to do some fast explaining to her husband, Fred. When she'd told him years before that Neal was dead, she'd thought that she was through with her first husband. Several years had passed with no contact, or at least no verifiable contact. Sometimes the telephone would ring three times, his old signal, and then it would be silent, and she felt that it was his way of letting her know that he was still watching. But leave it to Bill and his flare for the dramatic to come roaring back into her life on her birthday.

She was outside on the porch of her Tennessee home when Fred opened the screen door and called to her. "I need to tell you something," he said with a strange look on his face. One of Bill's sisters had just called, he said, "about Bill."

Oh, my God, he really is dead, she thought.

"I don't know how to tell you this," Fred said softly, "but he just killed three women."

Wilson fell to her knees and threw up. Guilt rose around her like the stench from her vomit. She recalled his threat to "fuck over every woman in my path." She'd believed him, but she'd always thought that he meant that he'd ruin women financially and emotionally, as he'd done to her. Never had it crossed her mind that he would kill someone. Now she knew that she'd been blind to the real man beneath the sweet smile and charm. *I knew it. I knew it.* She sobbed at the thought.

Over the next two weeks, Wilson wallowed in guilt. She begged God to forgive her for not watching Neal, not warning other women to stay away from him. She'd think of a hundred ways that she wished she'd killed him when she had the chance, and then ask God for forgiveness for wishing him dead.

She was afraid. If he'd killed these women, maybe he'd come after her. Not personally, he was in jail. But he knew *everybody,* had known how to find her when he wanted to, even knew what she was doing. She sent her daughter off to camp for two weeks, in case someone came to the house meaning harm.

She told the investigators that she knew how he had lured his victims. First there was the charm—the bubble baths, the roses, the extravagant gifts, and, most of all, the promises of a bright future. He knew instinctively what each woman wanted most—whether it was love, security, excitement, or just someone to listen—and then exploited their vulnerabilities.

Wilson wished that she'd been there to warn Rebecca Holberton, Candace Walters, and Angela Fite. "I would have told them: 'If you ever meet a man named William Lee Neal, turn and run the other way.' " But now it was too late.

The third wife, Karen Boxer, told them she'd met Neal in the early 1980s when she was living in Virginia. She was dating another man at the time, who was working for Neal's security systems company. She thought of her boyfriend's employer as "a very creative person" who knew how to treat women right. He tried to teach her boyfriend his gentlemanly ways—unfortunately, she recalled, to little effect.

Neal always had a large bankroll on him and seemed to like wearing tuxedos and riding around town in limousines. But she had little contact with him because he was always traveling. She broke up with her boyfriend and didn't see Neal for several years.

That's why, she said, she was surprised when he called her out of the blue at work sometime in 1986 or 1987, after his divorce from Karen Wilson. They started dating, but it wasn't a normal relationship. He would leave for a week or more at a time without telling her or even leaving a note saying when he'd be back.

"He was very controlling," Boxer told the investigators. He separated her from her family and friends, and in 1988 he insisted that they move to Colorado, where he worked for Denver Burglar Alarm.

He told her about his first two wives, always claiming to be the victim of their lies and infidelities. She knew that inside, Neal was "full of rage." One day he'd found his vehicle had been vandalized and he punched the curb so hard that he badly damaged his hand. He also seemed to cry at "inappropriate" times, but for the most part was able to control his emotions.

One day when they were arguing, she told him to leave. "And that really pushed his button." He pushed her against a wall and started choking her.

Nevertheless, when he proposed that they go to Alaska, where he had supposedly been stationed in the army, and get married, she accepted. She had always wanted to go to Alaska. They were married on September 10, 1989, in Portage, and spent two weeks there on their honeymoon before returning to Denver.

Neal was quite the outdoorsman, she told the

investigators, and dressed the part of "a mountain man" in flannel shirts and jeans, though he still liked going out dressed in a tuxedo. She never saw him as a cowboy.

In October, only a few weeks after returning from Alaska, he decided that it was time to return to Virginia. That move was followed in March 1990 by a move to Clifton Park, New York. He just couldn't seem to settle down and would reach his decisions suddenly and without notice.

When they were dating, he spent a lot of money on flowers and gifts for her. After their marriage, she told him to quit wasting their money, that it wasn't necessary. His whole demeanor seemed to change. He was often withdrawn and emotionally abusive, once calling her mother to report that she "sucks her thumb and sleeps in the fetal position." On one other occasion, he shoved her roughly up against a wall and put his hand over her mouth as if to smother her.

With her marriage heading downhill, Boxer wanted to try counseling, but Neal wouldn't go and was paranoid about what was being said about him when she went alone. They finally separated in November 1990. On that day, Neal called the New York State Police Department and told them that she was suicidal.

Boxer explained that she was plenty angry when he called the police, but "I was not suicidal." The police, however, made her go see a counselor at the hospital anyway. She never went to the "loony bin," as Neal had told his fourth wife, Jennifer Tate, but she did see another counselor to deal with issues from the marriage, including blaming herself "entirely" for the breakup.

When Neal left, he took more than her heart. He also took out cash advances on her credit cards totaling $9,000 and another $1,500 out of her savings account. Because they were still officially married at the time, she couldn't recoup her losses. It made one of his favorite sayings all the more bitter: "Anybody stupid enough to believe me deserves to get fucked."

Boxer warned the investigators that Neal was such a good con artist, she was sure that he would beat the system, even on this case. "I just knew I would see Bill's name in the headlines someday for something like this," she said.

Talking to Neal's fourth wife, Jennifer Tate, the investigators heard more of the same, though the sexual aggressiveness seemed to have increased. Otherwise, the women's stories had many similarities to those that the investigators were hearing of his activities in Denver, down to favorite sayings, such as: "Anybody stupid enough to believe me deserves to get fucked." None of them found the violence out of character—extreme, perhaps, unimaginable in its brutality and consequence, but not out of character . . . just the logical conclusion for a man who seemed to have spent his adult life manipulating and testing the women he supposedly loved, a man ruled by his insecurities and jealousies, his obsessions and paranoia. A man given to fits of rage at the drop of a hat . . . or a test failed. To a woman, they were worried that he would find a way to hurt them from behind walls and razor wire.

Neal's family had called Tate on Thursday, July 9, and told her of his arrest. Although she was in frequent contact with them, she hadn't seen her former husband since March 1995. He'd paid fairly regularly the child support that he owed, but she never heard anything else from him.

Neal's sister Peggy called and told her to watch the evening news. The next day, Tate went to see him at the jail. For all she had been through, she still couldn't believe that he would kill. When she saw him, she was taken aback by how terrible he looked in the bright orange jail jumpsuit that he was wearing. He was haggard and pale, with dark circles under his eyes.

"Oh, my little Baby Half-pint. I've always loved you, Baby Half-pint," he moaned as the tears welled in his blue eyes. He choked up over the words of how much he missed and needed her.

She didn't respond the way he would have liked. "Why'd you do it?" she asked, angry. "You had everything. You can do anything."

Neal stopped whining and looked at her coldly. The tears were gone. He shrugged. He had loved them all, he said, just like he had loved her. "But that's what happens when you fuck with me."

Twelve

"You have the right to remain silent. Anything you say can and will be used against you in a court of law.

"You have the right to speak with a lawyer and have him present during questioning. If you cannot afford a lawyer, the court will appoint one for you free of charge . . . which they've already done."

Investigator Jose Aceves read the Miranda advisory to the prisoner in the small interview room at the Jefferson County Detention Center. William Lee Neal had called asking to talk without his lawyer, Jim Aber, whom he'd fired for the television cameras and later reconsidered, being present and waived his rights immediately when they arrived that morning, as he was anxious to get to "the truth." Neal probably had already dug his own grave with his tape-recorded confession and statements that he'd made to investigator Cheryl Zimmerman, as well as several he'd made since to the police and media. But Aceves, a short, barrel-chested detective with jet-black hair and a Fu Manchu mustache who'd been the lead investigator at the West Chenango scene, and

Zimmerman, a nine-year veteran who'd talked Neal into surrendering and was also present in the interview room, were taking no chances that this interview would be tossed out on a technicality. There were still a lot of questions that they wanted to ask Wild Bill Cody Neal.

For one thing, they were still unclear regarding how he knew the victims, and whether the victims knew each other. And what ruse had he used to get them all into the town house on West Chenango?

There was also a question as to whether he had committed other murders. He'd claimed to have killed as many as "five hundred others" and that there were bodies that they had not yet discovered. He'd retracted the statements, but they had to assume that he might have been telling them the truth, or at least some of the truth, before changing his mind. No one believed his more fantastic claims, but he had proven he was quite capable of killing multiple victims over a period of time. It was also difficult to believe that at age forty-two he'd suddenly "snapped," as he now claimed, and started cooly, calmly murdering innocent women. The crimes seemed too well planned and calculated for a first-timer.

Three were dead and whatever the investigators knew about their relationship with him came from the women's families. The fourth woman, the one he'd raped, had told them how he'd brought her into the town house with a ruse about showing her a "surprise" for her roommate. In graphic detail, she had recounted his cold-blooded efficiency in killing the third victim, Angela Fite, and lack of remorse—while they shook their heads over the courage she had

Victim Rebecca Holberton, 42.
(Photo courtesy Jefferson County District Court)

Holberton lived in a rural community northwest of Denver. *(Photo courtesy Jefferson County District Court)*

Candace Walters *(left)* and her daughter Holly. *(Photo courtesy Jefferson County District Court)*

Victim Candace Walters, 48.
(Photo courtesy Jefferson County District Court)

Victim Angela Fite, 28. *(Photo courtesy Betty Von Tersch)*

Angela Fite *(right)*, 10, and her sister Tara, 7.
(Photo courtesy Betty Von Tersch)

Fite at 13 years old.
(Photo courtesy Betty Von Tersch)

Angela Fite *(right)* with her mother, grandmother, and baby son in June 1993. *(Photo courtesy Betty Von Tersch)*

Fite *(right)* and her mother Betty Von Tersch at Christmas in 1995. *(Photo courtesy Betty Von Tersch)*

Police scaled fence at the back of Holberton's town house so they could look through sliding glass doors.

Police outside Holberton's town house where murders took place. *(Photo courtesy* Denver Post*)*

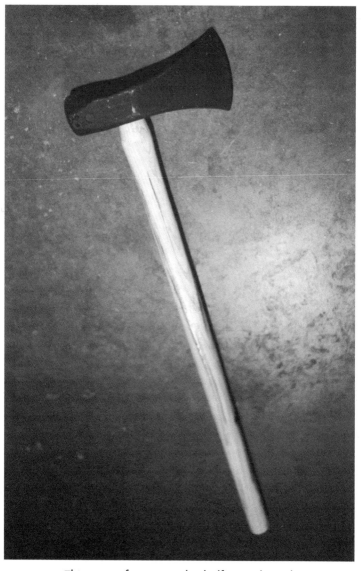

This type of seven-and-a-half-pound maul
was used to kill the three women.

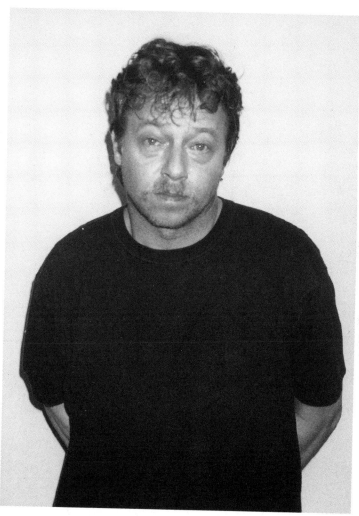

On July 8, 1998, William Cody Neal, 42, was taken into custody after telling police he had killed Holberton, Walters, and Fite. (Photo courtesy Jefferson County District Court)

With a kitten in his pocket *(right)* Wild Bill Cody Neal
poses for camera wearing his black Stetson
and long duster in 1998.
(Photo courtesy Jefferson County District Court)

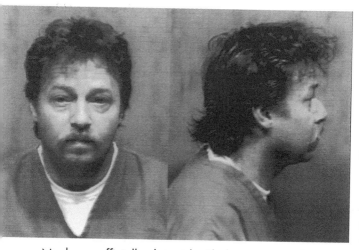

Neal was officially charged with three counts of
first-degree murder, first-degree kidnapping,
and first-degree sexual assault.
(Photo courtesy Jefferson County Sheriff's Department)

Neal at his death penalty hearing in Jefferson County
District Court in September 1999.
(Photo courtesy George Kochaniec, Jr., Rocky Mountain News)

Jefferson County Prosecutor Chris Bachmeyer.

Jefferson County District Attorney Dave Thomas.

Jefferson County Chief
Deputy District Attorney
Mark Pautler.

Jefferson County
Deputy District Attorney
Charles Tingle.

Jefferson County
Sheriff's Investigator
Jose Aceves.

Jefferson County
Sheriff's Investigator
Cheryl Zimmerman
Moore.

Angela Fite was buried in Denver, Colorado.
(Photo courtesy Betty Von Tersch)

shown throughout the ordeal. But she knew little about him.

The necessity of learning more about his past would be important if Neal was convicted and then faced a death penalty hearing. At such a hearing, defense lawyers would be expected to present evidence of "mitigating circumstances"—or mitigators—in their attempt to save his life. Mitigators often involved such explanations for criminal behavior as an abused childhood, physical injury that might have caused brain damage, or even a defendant's youth and lack of prior criminal history or history of violence. Neal was already claiming that his brutality was out of character for him, perhaps a first step toward an insanity plea.

The investigators had learned a lot about Neal's past and character from his family. He'd been born on October 7, 1955, in Virginia. His father had been in the air force and the family had soon moved to San Antonio, where he'd spent the better part of his youth. But he had been secretive from even his family for years.

One of his sisters, Sharon, a former social worker, was sticking by him . . . at least to the point of insisting that he must have been insane to do what he did and therefore not legally accountable for his actions. It was clear that she didn't want to provide any information that might harm her brother. But his other siblings— brother Phil and sister Peggy—were very helpful.

They described their brother as having spent his childhood as their mother's favorite, her "golden boy" who could do no wrong, even when as far back as his childhood there was plenty of evidence that he could. They reported instances of animal abuse, one of the telltale signs of a serial killer in the making. He'd claimed in an earlier interview with investigators to have been molested by an older, married woman while a young teen; his family, who knew the woman in question, patently denied the affair existed anywhere but in his mind. However, it was true that he had sexually molested a younger girl at about that age.

His second wife, Karen Wilson, had mentioned that while living with him near Nashville, Tennessee, there had been stories about murdered women whose bodies were found wrapped in plastic. They'd been unable to get anything concrete on that. Neal's own family revealed that he'd also been the subject of an investigation into the abduction, rape, and murder of a twelve-year-old girl in upstate New York many years before. The investigators knew that the FBI had been called in on that one, but Neal had denied any involvement, and without more to go on, he'd been free to walk. Even now, the police in Pueblo, 120 miles south of Denver, wanted to question Neal about a brutal murder there. But so far, they had not been able to link any more unsolved homicides or disappearances to Neal. So far.

A week after his arrest, Neal had been charged by Jefferson County District Attorney Dave Thomas with thirteen crimes, including first-degree murder, first-degree sexual assault, kidnapping, extortion, and theft. Though it might have seemed like overkill, considering a conviction for first-degree murder could result in the death penalty, proving the lesser charges might bear on whether Neal would qualify for the "ultimate punishment" due to his having committed the murders either during, or to conceal, another felony.

Neal had kept Jim Aber as his public defender for the time being, though he frequently threatened to fire him for trying to defend him from the charges. Not that Neal paid much attention to his lawyer's advice. He was bound and determined to take "full responsibility," as if that were some noble gesture on his part.

As Jose Aceves finished reading Neal his rights, the killer nodded impatiently. "I understand that fully, and I agree with it." He looked pale in the fluorescent lighting and a bright orange jail jumpsuit. He still wore his hair long, though he'd added a dark goatee since his arrest two months earlier.

"Did anyone from our office ask you to come talk to us?" Aceves asked.

"No, not at all," Neal replied.

"Mr. Neal, you haven't been threatened or coerced in any way to come down and talk to us?"

"No, no, sir," Neal said, shaking his head. "This is totally voluntary, not out of fear or anything like that. You guys have totally respected me the whole time I've been with you. That's another reason why I'm comfortable in talking with you . . . because of how you have handled things with me during this time that we've been in this situation."

Neal began the interview trying to butter up Cheryl Zimmerman by complimenting her on her appearance. But she cut quickly to the chase. "What is it you wanted to talk about, sir?"

First Neal cryptically said that he hoped they would get a message through to an agent with the FBI "relating to certain, what I believe are federal, issues, if worse comes to worse, if I don't have any other choice. I am considering what I'd like to say . . . and then they can do with the information whatever way they choose."

The investigators assured him that they'd been in contact with the FBI and would pass his messages along. But that wasn't their main concern. Zimmerman asked him to go over the day that Angela Fite had died.

Before he got started, Neal cautioned the investigators that he might not be able to remember everything "not because I'm hiding something. . . . It's just the act, I mean, the whole scene is such a nightmare to me as well."

Zimmerman asked him to try to remember the day at least from when he'd picked up Suzanne Scott. Neal described again how he'd asked her to go with him to the town house on the pretense of showing her "a surprise" for Beth Weeks. "I might have said I had something else to pick up at the house.

"I had a certain way that I wanted to—she was going to be the one presenting that surprise to Beth Weeks because I was going to be out of town to Vegas, and I wasn't going to be able to do it for her.

"So that's why she was willing to let me blindfold her when we got into the garage, as well as put duct tape on her mouth, which I was gentle about doing. It was totally voluntary on her part as well."

"Were her hands bound in any way?" Zimmerman asked.

"Oh, no, no," Neal said. "She came of her own free will on the understanding that what we were doing was legitimate. I mean, you know, if

I had told her I'm going to take you to the house, and I'm going to tie you down, and I'm going to rape you, and you're going to witness a murder, she's not going to go." Seeing the look on Aceves's face, he added, "I mean, I'm not being sarcastic with you at all, Jose."

Neal said he led the way into the house because "I was always so worried about the little kitty cat getting out."

Scott trusted him enough, he said, that she lay down on the mattress without protesting. "I just said, 'This is how I want you to do the surprise with Beth.' . . . They always knew how crazy I was." Again catching the investigators' looks, he quickly added, "I don't mean crazy, I feel, in a bad way. I was always kind of like fun, and I would do things people wouldn't seem to do, just partying and enjoying myself." His unknowing victim didn't complain, either, when he tied her arms and legs down.

"So then you tied her up, and then what happened?" Zimmerman asked. So far, his story was the mirror image of Scott's.

"Then I started taking her blouse off," he said. "She felt at that time that she was going to be . . . I believe she felt like she was going to be raped."

"Did she say anything?"

Neal shrugged. "She muttered a few things like, 'No.' Or started to be upset. And I said, 'If you want to live, you're basically going to have to listen to what I have to say.' " He noted that he'd read Scott's statement to the police. "I would like to say that I believe that she was totally honest and totally accurate except for certain timing issues. . . . Like something comes to me . . . It might have been on the news or things

I've read that said Angela Fite watched me rape Suzanne Scott, which is totally not true. I had never done that to Angela, okay? . . . As far as the news, they don't have a stinking clue, all right?"

"They never do," Zimmerman agreed.

"You know," Neal said, "I'm facing death row. . . . I'm facing the end of my life for what I know that I've confessed, and I'm fine with doing that over and over again. I want the truth to be out. But I find it real difficult for me to see people, even my own flesh and blood, that have lied or added to something that was not true.

"I'm not saying that I'm always truthful with things. I mean, I have not been that way in my life. . . . I'm not trying to judge them, either, but I do have a problem with it, mainly because I believe it takes away from the investigation, and it's putting something on me I don't deserve. I'll eat what's mine but nothing else."

When the investigators began asking questions, they addressed him as Mr. Neal, until he insisted that they call him Cody. Some of their questions he answered directly; with others he took off on tangents—all the while, his hands flew around like a pair of disturbed birds. He would flit from subject to subject, often following no particular order and it was everything the investigators could do to keep him on track as he told his story. He described showing Scott the body of Rebecca Holberton covered in black plastic.

"Did you say anything to her at that point?" Zimmerman asked.

"I let her know that if she screamed or drew attention to herself, she would die," he answered. "She wasn't hysterical."

The investigators nodded; they were already duly impressed by how well Scott had held herself together under horrific circumstances. Still, Aceves thought that at some point after being shown Holberton's or Walters's body, the girl had screamed.

Neal shook his head. "She was not screaming. She never screamed the whole time she was with me. And if she recalls that she did, she did not.

"I mean, the only real tense time for Suzanne with me was in the beginning when I got on top of her, and I settled her down right away. And then I took the blindfold off to reassure her that murder was definitely an option. I wanted her to live, and she was going to have to trust me that she would live. But she was going to have to follow exactly what I said."

"What was her reaction to seeing these two people?" Zimmerman asked.

"I'm not a doctor," Neal noted. "Just my observation was I believe that she was in shock, but not bad shock. She was still in control of her senses. She was aware of what was going on." He took a deep breath and added, "I believe part of it is because Suzanne trusted that I would get her out of there alive, even after she saw the bodies."

Neal said he removed the duct tape from Scott's mouth so that she could talk to him. "So that I could understand, you know, what she's going through a little bit more. I mean, I know that might sound bizarre to you, my concern for a victim, but believe me it was a concern because she was a beautiful young lady. She never did nothing wrong to me at all."

If Neal's rationale sounded bizarre to the investigators, they didn't let it show on their faces. "Why did you choose to do this to Suzanne?" Aceves asked.

"As a warning," Neal answered. "And at this time, I don't want to go further into that, but it was a warning to other people to keep their mouths shut."

Aceves pressed to know who these other people might be and why they needed to be warned. But Neal was coy and refused go any further, other than to say the investigators "should be concerned." There was a strong possibility, he said dramatically, that he was "going to get hit. And I have a real concern about it. Not because I'm scared to die. It's not that. But I'm scared that I'll die before I can get the truth out." His warning, he said, was meant for some of his acquaintances, especially Jimmy Gerloff. "I hope he takes it serious and you do; this way I wash my hands of it. I can't be there to protect him. . . . I believe there's a possibility Jimmy Gerloff will die, and I don't want that on me." He hinted darkly that some of the danger might be connected to the drug trade.

Neal turned to the matter of picking up Angela Fite that evening at Fiddlesticks. It was his suggestion, he said, that she take the kids to the baby-sitter before meeting him. "I wanted to make sure the children were in no way directly involved in the scene. And I'd like to make a statement for the record for myself to you that there was no intention of harming Kayla or Kyle in any way. The purpose in getting them to the baby-sitter was to make sure some adult was taking good care of them so that they were not involved in this thing with Angie."

Having tried to make himself sound somehow noble for not involving the children, he told the investigators that when Angie got into his truck for the drive to the town house, he told her that she was going to "meet some friends, family, and that we were going to go over to this house that I had talked to her about."

The investigators were curious though about who the mysterious friends and family might have been. Neal avoided those questions and noted that he'd also led her to believe that she was going to own the town house. "I let her know with what I said that I did not want anyone knowing, her family or her friends or Matt or anybody other than herself knowing that she was going to be getting a house. That she would die if she disclosed that information."

Beth Weeks told investigators that Neal had said to her that he'd killed Fite because she was reconciling with Matt Rankin. But Neal denied that he was jealous. He said that he'd told Fite that "if her and Matt ended up wanting to get back together, that was fine," but he didn't want anybody to know that the house was coming from him.

"And what I found out before she died was that she had been running her mouth about that and a few other things as well. And that's one of the reasons why Angie died. Fair warning. . . . She brought up that she didn't believe that I was totally legit, meaning that I was involved in bad things. She said she had been around things because of Matt's jail record and things . . . that she could handle it, and that she would never disclose anything that her and I did.

"Candace never saw Rebecca's body, you see,

before she died because she would have leapt out of there and fought like a cat.

"But Angie, I allowed her to see it and also see that there was somebody there living. I wanted to confront her. She was going to die for opening her mouth. . . . That's why Jimmy Gerloff is going to die, and that won't be because I'm the one. If I could stop it right now—that's what I'm trying to do—I would do it."

Neal claimed that he told Fite, "Because you're a snitch, you die" before he killed her. It was a claim that he'd never made before and one that Scott had not remembered. He continued with his new fantasy of having given fair warning. "I mean, I can't give you any clearer warning than that. And she did, and she died."

Aceves interrupted. The investigator wanted to pin Neal down on his frame of mind at the time of the killing, an important issue when trying to convict him of premeditated first-degree murder. "What's going through your mind?"

"I'm very clear and calm," Neal replied. "I was totally comfortable." When he was out picking up Fite, he was a little worried about Scott being discovered, "but I wasn't bouncing off the wall. . . . Angie couldn't even tell anything was wrong with me."

"Was it like an adrenaline rush?" Aceves asked.

"No, it wasn't an adrenaline rush there," he said. "The adrenaline rush would come when I would kill somebody, like being a Highlander." (*Highlander* was a movie and television show in which the hero, an immortal who has been alive for hundreds of years, must fight other immortals who sought to absorb his life force and he theirs.) "You know, he feels when he just sits there and he kills somebody, and he raises his hand.

"I'm not being funny about it. I'm just saying that in order for me to deal with killing . . ." Neal stopped and searched for the right words. "These three murders were not like that with me, OK? This was different to me, all right? Because I cared about them."

Zimmerman asked if he thought that he was a controlling person. "You know, I'm learning about that issue right now," he said, nodding. He said that he'd read where his sister Peggy told the investigators that "nobody controls Bill," and acknowledged that was probably correct.

"But I don't think in an evil sense. I'm a strong-willed person. I mean, if somebody has to make a decision, let it be me, because right or wrong, I'm going to make it. Somebody has got to be a leader."

"That's right," Zimmerman agreed, wanting him to go on.

"I was trained that way," Neal boasted. "But I was also hurt that way, being a sheep and taking it and then saying: 'Enough, I'm not [to] be led no more. Nobody is going to rape me no more. Nobody is going to hurt me no more. Nothing. OK? And if you do, you die."

Neal changed the subject to note that he wasn't happy with some of the things that he'd been reading in the press about his case, or some of the things that his family and past acquaintances had told the police. He said that it was the press who misrepresented his service record, contending that he never told reporters that he was a member of the elite Airborne Rangers, something that had since been disproved. "I said I was with an Airborne Ranger company," he said. "I didn't lie. I was there and trained with them and went to the field with them. I did everything while waiting to go to Ranger school."

Neal said his army career was cut short when he was only seventeen after being raped by his sergeant. The incident, he claimed, happened one evening after he'd returned to the barracks following a hard day in the field. "I was exhausted, and he told me I could finally lay down and go to sleep. I was lying on my stomach, and I woke up to having him on top of me."

Neal said that he didn't want to discuss what happened any further. He noted that while Suzanne would be "getting therapy for a long, long time" for what he had done to her, nobody had ever offered the same counseling to him. It was because of the rape, he said, that he decided to drop the Airborne Ranger idea and go elsewhere. "Because of the rape, I chose to go elsewhere because everybody was calling me a faggot and I was fighting. I was beating people up."

The rape in the army wasn't the first time he'd been sexually assaulted, Neal said, getting back to the story of the older, married woman who'd taken advantage of him as a boy. There'd also been a minister who molested him. He conceded again that he'd turned the tables and molested a younger girl.

After several hours, Neal asked for a coffee break. When they returned and the tape recorder started up again, Neal asked the investigators how they could sleep at night. "I'm not trying to be nosy or disrespectful," he said. "It's just that, you know, it's enough of a horror for me, let alone what you see in your everyday jobs."

Aceves shrugged. "You deal with it and you do what you need to do," he said. "It's part of your job, and you learn to keep it separate from your home life."

Neal nodded. "This past couple of months has been a real eye-opener for me," he said. "But I haven't run from it. That's one thing they'll never take from me. I didn't run from it." He congratulated the investigators on their professionalism, but he did wish that the next time they met, they'd bring him a pack of cigarettes. Merit 100s. He promised he would "really open up" if they brought the cigarettes.

Zimmerman cut through the banter by asking Neal to tell her, "Who is Cody? . . . I want to know the whole story. You know, part of it is my own personal curiosity. . . . There's a lot that's gotten you to this point in your life. We can get some of it from other people—family, friends, your military records, and so on. But there's a lot of it, Cody, that I can't get except out of your head and your heart."

Neal liked this approach. He nodded and, choking up, said, "I want that, to be honest with you."

Aceves jumped in, saying that the FBI wasn't going to get more involved unless Neal could "throw them a bone," give them some exact incidents rather than just his hints that there might have been other crimes, other victims.

Neal hedged. He wanted all that, too, he said. But he had other things to consider . . . other lives and the possibility that the police would "drop the ball" and the truth would be lost.

Whatever that meant. He said that he couldn't talk to his defense lawyer "about all of this because he's trying to defend me.

"I need prosecution. I need justice to be served because I'm representing three dead people, as well as a rape victim. I want justice to be served and the truth to be known so that people can get on with their lives. And that's why we're here today."

Aceves tried to steer Neal back to how he was able to get the women to trust him so well. "Cody, you mentioned control. . . . How did Cody manage to control?"

Neal replied that he sometimes controlled people by molding himself to be what they wanted or needed him to be. "It's like if you want a raise, you're going to have to look a certain way, do your job a certain way, smile at a certain person instead of saying, 'You stinkin' asshole' when you want to. Or you let somebody think you like them when you don't. . . . I mean, an illusion, taking advantage, finding a weak point in a human being—you know, greed, lust . . . to get my own way."

Zimmerman asked what weaknesses he found in Rebecca Holberton, but Neal shook his head. "I don't want to talk about Rebecca Holberton at this time, OK?" he said, his voice cracking with emotion.

"Were you closer to her than the others?"

"Oh, yeah," he replied. "I don't want to lose it talking about Rebecca." But, of course, then he went on and talked about her. He claimed that they had sex at the party where they met, and he moved into her town house on West Chenango Drive soon thereafter. Four months later, the relationship was no longer sexual. They sometimes still shared the same bed, or he'd sleep downstairs, he said, "but we were just friends."

"What was Candace's weakness?" Zimmerman asked. "I mean, what did you find weak about her that you could manipulate?"

Neal hesitated, then said, "First of all, I'm not saying that I manipulated Candace Walters, OK? I honestly liked Candace Walters, and I'm talking about at the beginning when I met her.

"I found her to be a charming lady, along with the other bartenders that have worked there. We had a really beautiful conversation just sitting in that little booth there when she was off. . . . She was easy to talk to. Then as I got to know her, I found a very troubled person, which I could relate to because I've been very troubled in my life, too."

"What do you think she was troubled about?" Zimmerman asked.

"I think she was troubled about men . . . how she had been treated by them in the past. . . . She had told me she had been raped. . . . Whether you want to believe that or not, I'll swear to [it] that Candace felt she was raped by Jimmy Gerloff." He said the accusation was a warning to Gerloff. "Jimmy, you've got to own up. You did something you shouldn't have done with a woman that said no and meant no. No means no."

Aceves steered him back to how he controlled Walters.

"Candace saw me with a lot of money," he answered. "I always like throwing it and giving it because I remember what it felt like when I didn't have it. . . . And look at me now, you know, I can't hardly even get a stinkin' stamp. All those people I took care of, and then where are they? I mean, nowhere. They're like, poof, gone, including my family. Steve Grund . . . He promised to be over here, and he ain't here, OK?"

The investigtors noted that Grund and the others might be witnesses in the case and therefore shouldn't have contact with him. Neal said he'd thought that might be the reason, too.

In the beginning, he only intended his relationship with Walters to be a "platonic friendship." He was not sexually attracted to her. But after the incident with Gerloff, both to protect his friend and to show Walters that "not all men are pigs," he took her to a hotel room and treated her to a bubble bath. "And there was no sexual contact that night."

The relationship changed, Neal said, after Walters began "stalking" him. "She started calling me more, paging me and paging me." He took that as a type of threat. "Then eventually her and I had sex. But it wasn't attraction sex to me. It was like me as a . . . almost like a sexual slave, saying: 'I'm going to do this. I'm going to do this woman just to give her what she wants to get her out of my life,' OK?

"Eventually, it just kept getting worse. She wouldn't take no for an answer with me. It was almost like a fatal attraction."

"Of those three women, Rebecca, Candace, and Angie—" Zimmerman had started to say.

"Yes," Neal anticipated.

"Which one do you think you were the most attracted to?"

"Angie," he answered almost before she finished the question. "Rebecca and I had a sexual relationship, but I was too much for Rebecca."

Suddenly Neal said he had to use the rest room. "If I don't go," he said with a grin, "I'm going to be doing your carpet."

When he returned, Aceves wanted to read him his rights a second time.

"Do we have to go through that again?" Neal protested. "I'm fine with talking to you guys."

But Zimmerman picked up where her partner left off. "You realize you have the right to your lawyer at any time you want. And you have the right to stop at any time you like."

Neal sighed. "Yes." He looked at Aceves, who was Hispanic, and asked him if there was American Indian in his family. "Do you know about covering tracks?" he said. "I was good at covering things or putting so much shit out, pardon the French, that everybody—they thought they knew me, and they ain't even stinking close. They don't even know the first color of my hair. How do you know this ain't dyed?"

Zimmerman replied, "I think I've heard you had blond hair for a while."

Neal smiled. He could change his appearance easily, he said. "I'm growing a goatee," he said, then teased, "It's for me escaping, you see." The investigators looked surprised. He quickly added, "I'm just kidding."

He said that he'd once grown a goatee when his mother was in the cancer ward before her death. "I said I wasn't going to shave my goatee until she was in the Lord's arms. And she said, 'You and Sir Walter Raleigh.'" His mother had asked him then to get her out of the ward, so he took her home to die. "So that's why I'm growing this is because I plan on dying. Chances are I'll be executed for this one. I deserve to be, not because I'm suicidal, I'm not.

"If I end up being that way, I know the people to call because I plan on going to Heaven, all right? That's just my own religious belief. I do, because He'll forgive those things. I mean, you know, it's like you hear . . . the jailhouse thing: you get in trouble and you go to God. Well, that's sometimes the only time that He's able to get through your skull, all right?"

Neal hesitated when asked more about his relationship with his mother. "My mother killed me, OK, period," he said as he choked up and wiped tears from his eyes.

"What do you mean she killed you?" Zimmerman asked.

"It's love," he sniffed. "You've just got to not talk about my mom." He stopped, unable to go on. At last he whispered, "Let me catch my breath, OK? Do you mind? I'm sorry, I just, I don't have a lot of patience for a lot of emotion with all the weight that I got on me."

With a little prompting from the investigators, however, he admitted that after his mother's death, he forged two checks against her account and stole some of her jewelry—because his siblings were "trying to cheat me. My mother let me know that they were going to write my ass off as soon as she was dead. Meaning she was the only thing that was keeping the wolves away from these greedy little children she had. She asked me what things of hers I wanted. And I said, 'All I want is you, Mom.' And that's honestly what I wanted. I didn't want her money or her furniture. I wanted my mother living, OK?"

If his mother were still alive, he said, she would have been there for him "in a heartbeat" despite what he'd done. "Now she would not pat me on the back. She wouldn't dance and kick her heels. She would not say, 'You did the right thing, killing those people.' It would have probably killed her, but she would have still stood with me."

Neal said that his mother had died on October 11, 1995, "just prior to me meeting Candace." He wiped again at his eyes and apologized for the emotional display.

Zimmerman commiserated. "There's nothing wrong with it, Cody."

Aceves asked Neal if he believed his own lies. "No," Neal replied. "I know the truth, all right? You know, my brother was the one that said, my brother, Phil, and I love him dearly, that I couldn't con him. That's bullshit. I've been conning him all my life."

Neal promised that he was going to "separate for you what's lies and what is the truth. And I will tell you that I have told you some hellacious lies at times, all right, to cover my ass, so I don't disclose other areas that I don't want you looking in yet, OK?"

The prisoner kept diverting into vague generalities, but the investigators pressed on. Aceves asked Neal how he was making a living in 1998.

"All the money I was getting was illegal," Neal replied. He claimed to have been a cat burglar who stole jewelry, diamonds, and gold from stores and homes but would supply no specifics.

"Did Rebecca know that you were taking money out of her account?"

"Oh, yeah," he answered. "She would make checks out to me, and I would cash them."

When Aceves asked how much money he'd stolen from Holberton, Neal stalled. The detective pressed and the prisoner growled, "Be careful how many times you ask me for more, all right?"

Neal immediately thought better of copping an attitude, saying that he didn't mean to be aggressive, and admitted to "better than twenty grand." Aceves wasn't letting him off so easy: "Based on our investigation, Cody, is it more like fifty, sixty grand?"

"It could be, sir," Neal replied. He would need to spend some time focusing on Holberton to make sure that was accurate, he added.

Neal said that he was trying to avoid a jury trial because it might reflect on his victims' reputations. "The public deserves to know there was a crime committed, and that I'm guilty," he said. "But they don't need to know about Rebecca's sexual habits or how dirty she liked keeping her town home. . . . I wasn't the only pig, OK?"

The money he used for strip clubs and limousines: "I think the only month that I ever counted how much money I blew in a month was twenty-two thousand dollars at a strip club. Just like, poof." He boasted that he'd throw money over the rail onto the dance floor at the country-western bar, The Stampede, and laughed at the people below scrambling to pick up the money. "Then they'd look up and they'd see me there with some beautiful babes. See, people don't want to be down there picking. . . . The smart ones don't want to pick it up; they want to have it to throw.

"And then when I would throw that money,

it's like an investment. I would take a chance. I would throw this money, and a victim would come up, somebody that I could use, manipulate, get more money out of, you see?"

Neal admitted to taking money from Holberton's account on the day that she died. Aceves asked him what it was used for and he replied, "Luring Suzanne and Angie and finishing this thing."

He'd been thinking of how to carry out the murders for a week, maybe two, before he put his plan into effect. Part of what put him into "a tailspin," as Aceves had described it, was being "stalked" by Candace Walters, though he denied that he was worried about Walters's threat to contact Holberton, who was just a roommate, he'd told her, not a lover. "I warned Candace if she kept pressing it, she was going to die, OK? And Candace wouldn't let go, man. She would not let up. She wanted a piece of my ass."

The rumor that she wrote a letter in case something happened to her, Neal complained, was another instance of Walters breaking her promise not to talk about him. He said Walters was too angry to take his threat seriously.

A more important reason for the murder of Holburton, he claimed, was actually an act of kindness. He wanted the investigators to know, "I was never mean to Rebecca, never hurt Rebecca, never beat on her."

In fact, he was doing Holberton a favor when he killed her. "I was trying to spare Rebecca the nightmare that her financial world might be coming to a close. Not that she was totally going to die, just her financial stability. She worked all her life to have that. . . . She was greedy; she

wanted to retire from the phone company." She
had about $40,000 in taxes due that August and
"Rebecca was going to wake up to this one-hun-
dred-thousand-dollar nightmare and never be
able to pay it back until she was sixty-five. She
was going to be a slave. And, you know, I grieve
over that."

Aceves asked Neal how he viewed his sexuality.

"I don't have a healthy sexuality," Neal answered, "and I don't believe that anybody could
after being raped or molested, all right? I don't
even know what normal is; I haven't known what
normal is since childhood."

"Do you feel a hatred towards women?"
Aceves asked.

Neal furrowed his brow. "No, not that I am
aware of," he said, then paused before adding,
"I mean, it's not in my conscious mind. A psychiatrist might say deep down I hate women."

"Do you have a hatred towards men who like
other men based on what's happened to you?"

"Oh, I did," Neal agreed. "My brother will tell
you I hated homosexuals with a passion."

"You were never homosexual prior to the—"
Aceves didn't get to finish his question.

Neal was angry. "Never," he growled. "Uh-uh.
Hell no! No way!" But he quickly calmed down.
To prove his point, he boasted that he lost count
of his female sexual conquests "at a thousand"
while still in his midtwenties.

Zimmerman asked if, perhaps, he was bitter
toward Fite because she was trying to reconcile
with Matt Rankin. Neal shook his head. "Angie
didn't die because she went and spent the night
with Matt. That is not why Angie died, all right?

"I've had my wives. . . . All except for one wife

cheated on me, OK? But Angie didn't die because she cheated on me."

One of his ex-wives, Jennifer Tate, he said, was lying to them when she claimed that he'd made almost no attempt to see their little girl since their breakup. "She has never let me see her," he contended. "I have tried over and over again to see her. She is a liar. She has always punished me, thinking I cheated on her. She doesn't deserve to be with me. I want to be free to do my shit."

Neal described himself as loyal and felt bad that he "cheated" on Angie with Beth Weeks; he was also an attentive and sensitive lover. "Look, I'm not a womanizer. I'm not here to use you sexually. I have feelings and care for you, but if you think I'm using you and just sleeping with everybody else, take yourself and your bad ass out of here. I'm not here just for a piece of ass. I'm here for somebody to love me and love somebody else one on one.

"I was sensitive to them. I wouldn't ask them to do something they didn't like. But because of my experiences sexually, I could take them wherever they wanted to go and bring them back. I mean, I've been very open-minded with sex, or I would have been a stinking rapist and raping women, you know, and murdering them like Ted Bundy, so to speak, all through the years.

"I raped a woman. . . . If Suzanne were the only crime I ever did in my life, I would hope you would execute me for it. That's how I feel about rape, OK? It was so wrong. Nor, like I told her, would it happen again. Nor am I a rapist. I don't believe that I would ever rape another woman after the taste that I got on this issue, all right? It's something that I can never feel like I've washed myself enough, just like them. I know what it felt like for it to happen to me. I felt dirty all my stinking life."

He denied that tying Suzanne Scott to the mattress was a "bondage" thing. "Understand, it was meant to restrain a victim." However, he conceded that he'd been into "light bondage" in the past.

Neal denied being sexually stimulated by the murders. "You know what?" he said, smiling as he shook his head. "That's the most off-the-wall question I could think of. But, I mean, I'm sure it's a good one in your business. First of all, murder and sex to me . . . I'm totally, like, 'Wow, man!' I mean, I never ever considered they go together . . . other than rape.

"It's not like I had a woody raising the ax up and killing them, all right? Waste another second on that and you're spinning your wheels. I executed them. I wanted them to go as quickly as possible.

"I was not thinking of sex in any way when I murdered Rebecca, Angie, or Candace. It had nothing to do with saying, 'Look, bitch, for all the other ones who cheated on me in the past.' . . . Now that would relate to sex. . . ."

Again Neal said that he "executed" his victims. "I wanted them to go as quickly as possible. And I believe that you both know that they had to have died very quick."

Actually, the investigators knew that Neal's assertion that his victims had died quickly with the first blow was not borne out by the examination of the bodies by forensic pathologist Ben Galloway. He did determine that Holberton probably died within the first few moments; the damage to her skull and brain had been devastating. However, Galloway had ascertained that both Candace Walters and Angela Fite had lived for several minutes after the attacks. How much pain they were feeling—what, if any, thoughts or fears may have gone through their minds—was anybody's guess.

Zimmerman asked why he had picked a maul as the murder weapon. "Why that versus just an ax or just a sledgehammer?"

"Well, you know, I don't know how to answer this," Neal answered. He pondered the question for a moment longer, then asked, "Have you ever murdered anybody?"

"No," Zimmerman replied.

"Have you?" he asked, turning to Aceves.

"No, I haven't," Aceves answered. "We just want to know why you chose a maul."

Neal reminded them that the murders were neither a "vindictive act" nor a "sexual act." "It was to put them out the best way I knew how, as quickly and as silently and as fairly as I could. . . . In fact, I believe, even though I haven't yet experienced lethal injection, it was a lot more compassionate and fair to kill them like that. Even though it didn't look real pretty, it was instant, OK?"

Demonstrating how he struck his victims, Neal raised his hands and brought them down in a chopping motion. "Meaning, *boom,* dead. And if they weren't dead and just throbbing, so to speak, they sure as hell weren't thinking about the pain."

"Did you think how many times you'd have to

hit them, Cody, in order to make it instant?"
Aceves said.

"I knew I had to make the first one count to
kill them right there . . . kill them and put them
unconscious," Neal answered.

"Did you have any idea where you had to hit
them?"

"Oh, I knew where I had to hit them. . . .
Where I was going was right dead center in the
top of the head at first blow."

"Always from the back?"

"Always from the back," he replied. "See, I
didn't want these people to know what was coming because they were good people. . . . It was a
mercy thing. It was, like, not wanting them to
suffer. The paper said I tortured them, OK. I
mean, if I wanted to torture them, I could have
sat there and, I mean, I could have done all
kinds of things. . . . I wanted them not to know.
I mean Rebecca and I had just finished some
champagne, you know; I had a surprise for her.
Same with Candace."

"And why the maul?" Zimmerman asked, coming back to her original question.

"Because it had weight to it. . . . I knew it
would be enough to kill."

Neal changed the subject. He wanted to set
the record straight regarding reports from his
family that he'd abused and killed small animals.
The police were interested in this facet as many
forensic psychiatrists maintain that there is a cor-
relation between a trio of behaviors during childhood and adolescence that might identify
potential serial killers. The three: bed-wetting,
fire setting, and cruelty to animals, often in con-
junction with sexual abuse.

The stories that his family told were half-truths and lies, he complained, such as the incident of him biting the head off a pet hamster. "The only hamster that I ever did kill was when I was older. It was a friend's pet, and I reached in to pet him and it bit me. . . . I didn't like meanness, ever. I'd had enough done to me. To protect myself, I went *boom*, like that, and killed him," he said, indicating that he punched the hamster.

"Did you ever abuse any cats or dogs?" Aceves asked.

"Well, hell, yeah," Neal replied as if that were a common behavior among all boys. But, he said, the story that his brother told them about pitch-forking a cat "because I felt like it . . . Well, that was either his poor memory or a lie to make me look worse than I was."

The truth, he said, was that "damn right I pitchforked that cat, all right? . . . I went in there and was going to pet the cat because I like animals. I always have. I pet them. I went over to pet him, and this cat tore into me. And my temper when I was young . . . Well, I grabbed this fork, and I just pitchforked this thing. . . . It's like they put animals to sleep for biting some-body. I mean, what's the difference? It attacked me; I defended myself; I killed it—simple as that."

Then there was the cat that was owned by a girlfriend. It used to "attack" his feet when he was sleeping. He warned the young woman that if the cat kept it up, "I was going to kill it. I don't never like anybody—and this is after I got out of the service—messing with me when I'm sleeping. Wake me up too sudden, you could ex-pect—I mean I would consider killing you." The unfortunate cat went after his feet again, so he grabbed his nunchakus—a martial arts weapon consisting of two sticks attached by a chain—and "tracked it down to the kitchen and killed it. And there was blood everywhere, man. . . . I told her to clean it up and went back to sleep."

Aceves asked if those were the only cats he'd killed. No, Neal admitted, there'd been others "who were mean to me."

Nor were the hamster and cats the only pets to suffer. "I had a dog that bit me one time, and I killed him, too. And then I had a puppy that bit me that I killed. The puppy was mean. It was just like something was wrong with him."

"How did you kill him?" Aceves asked.

"I punched his brain in," he said, "just, *boom!*"

His siblings said what they did because they were jealous of him, he said. "I was Mom's favorite. I could get away with murder. Now they're all stinkin' lying. What's new? Just like they want the electric chair to just get rid of me. Get what I deserve, right?"

However, he admitted that he'd continued killing animals as an adult, but that "killing animals was better than killing any more human beings, if that makes sense."

The investigators knew that Neal once had a job as a truck driver that had him crisscrossing the country. "While you were doing that, Cody, did you ever kill anyone on the road?" Aceves asked. "I mean, going from state to state, nobody would ever know that you were—"

"No, no." Neal shook his head. But, he added, it was a cover in case he had to "do some jobs."

Neal denied any extensive drug use. He'd used cocaine or methamphetamine in the past, but on an irregular basis. He did like to drink, boasting that he'd done as many as twenty-seven shots of tequila at a sitting. He also bragged about his fighting prowess, including an incident with Beth Weeks's husband before they were divorced. "I got him to where he got right in what I call my kill zone . . . close enough so I could chop him in the throat to finish him." Weeks and Gerloff had intervened.

Overall, Neal was defensive about his toughness. Since his arrest, he'd been kept in isolation at the jail, as he'd demanded as one of the conditions for his surrender. He told investigators that it was to prevent him from killing anyone else, but his jailers figured it had more to do with his fears of what might happen to him if he was placed in the general population. Rapists and woman killers were not popular, even among other criminals, and Neal was no imposing physical specimen.

The investigators noted that Neal had promised all three murder victims a house. "How many other women did you do that with?" Zimmerman asked.

"I'd have to think about that one," he replied. But first he wanted lunch and those cigarettes he'd asked for.

"Can I ask one more question?" Aceves asked.

"Yes, sir," Neal replied.

Aceves wanted to know what would have happened to the bodies of the three women if they hadn't been discovered on Wednesday. He was thinking of the two new footlockers and the unused saw next to them in the living room.

"I would like to answer that when we get off of break," Neal said, "because you're opening a real big door and probably one that's worth at least an hour to get cleared up easy, OK? They wouldn't have ended up being there. But then there would have been probably a bunch of other people killed that you don't know about."

Thirteen

When the trio met again after lunch, and the requested cigarettes, Jose Aceves made sure he had Cody Neal on the record again stating that it was his wish to speak to them without his lawyer. They did not immediately get back to what Neal had planned to do with the bodies.

Neal wanted to begin by "clearing up" some things about himself and Candace Walters. He wanted to make it clear that she did not try to blackmail him, "but she did threaten to go to the authorities." It was that or give her more of his time, he claimed.

"My look at it was: time was money as well as my life. It was something personal. I had already been raped when I was younger and molested . . . and this is not disrespectful to Candace . . . but I did not want to give myself physically to her."

Yes, he said, he was angry with her demands to get her money back. "But that's not why she died. I was angry with her because she wanted something out of me I didn't want to give to her, and that was my time . . . sex. . . . It's like, man, if I'm going to be a whore, let me get paid for it."

"Why did she lend the money to you?" Aceves asked.

"Because I let her know that I needed some money for some stuff regarding my little girl as a way to touch her," Neal replied with a shrug. "Also some trouble I was in in Las Vegas regarding borrowing money from somebody."

"And who was that from?" Cheryl Zimmerman asked.

"That was from nobody," Neal said. "It was a scam . . . a bullshit thing. I used that in order to manipulate to get something out of somebody."

Neal noted the deception with Chief Deputy District Attorney Mark Pautler posing as a public defender trying to arrange his surrender. The move was "inappropriate," he said, "but I believe that you did the right thing under the circumstances."

"Our whole concern that night was to get to you before somebody else got you," Aceves said.

"That's correct," Neal agreed. "And I still think that you were professional and did right by the community."

Suddenly Neal reversed himself on why Walters was murdered. "I killed Candace because she got to Rebecca." She'd found out where he lived about a month before the killings, he said, and talked to his roommate. "She was going to blow my cover."

"So what was it that Rebecca told you that Candace said to her?" Zimmerman asked.

"That I was a hit man—OK?—for the Mafia."

"And why did she tell her that?"

"Because she believed that I was."

"Cody, are you a hit man?"

Neal shook his head. "No, I'm not." He said that his world "was rapidly falling apart. . . . I mean, my covers, my bullshit, was catching up to me. And the reason was because of Candace stalking me. She was ruthless."

The matter came to a head when Rebecca told him that her taxes would be due in August and she would need her money. She believed that he had been using it for investments and to pay off loan sharks, never realizing that he'd spent most of it on one long party.

"Cody, was there anybody in Las Vegas that you really owed money to?" Zimmerman asked.

"No."

Aceves asked why he had urinated on Walters's body.

"Twice," Neal admitted, as the "ultimate humiliation. I just whipped it out, and it was basically around the shoulders and head. I urinated on her because, you know, 'Lady, you're gone. My life is gone. Rebecca. Angie. . . . Careful where you dig, OK? It was my way of also saying, 'Don't. I've had enough, people. You're backing me into a corner.'

"It was like an Oriental martial arts thing or an Indian thing. I mean, I hope somebody pisses on me when I'm gone, all right?"

He said that he hoped others would take it as a warning. He said that he needed to be kept separated from the other inmates. "An inmate was beating on my stinkin' door. I just photographed him in my head, just like, 'I'll remember you forever. And as soon as I'm out of this door, and I'm within striking distance, I'm going to kill you. . . . I've had enough.

"If I can murder someone I love, what am I going to do to some bastard that I don't love or have any respect for? I'm going to tear him up. Then you're going to know what torture is. . . . Disrespect me and abuse me, and then you're going to see it's like I'm two people, all right? The good and the bad, and then it gets real ugly."

Having made his point, Neal turned back to the murders, saying he loved "all three of those people. Candace was a good person. . . . She was a good soul and did not deserve to die.

"Nobody does. I don't even believe Ted Bundy deserved to die . . . or even me. But justice is justice." The difference between his victims and himself, he said, "was that I was judge, jury, and executioner all in one. I had no right to do that, but I gave fair warning."

Neal said that he was in a "normal, relaxed state" when he killed the women. "I wasn't angry to where I said, 'Fucking bitch . . .' *boom!* . . . I just totally knew where it was going. I knew, when it came down to it, I would not hesitate. It was just, *boom!*"

Nor did he disassociate during the murders. "If I had done that, I wouldn't have been able to hit the mark with that ax, like chopping wood. I knew that I could not slip with that first stroke. I had that thing in my hand not even maybe one second, two seconds, before it was in her brain and she was dead."

"Why didn't you use a gun?" Aceves asked.

"I didn't want to put a gun to their heads or a shotgun to the back of their heads and blow their heads off, because of the neighbors, you know. And then I would have had to kill the next-door neighbor and the painter and . . . It's like if the neighbor would have come over, I'd have killed the neighbor. I would have just gone ahead and went on a real killing spree. I mean, you guys would have had to pump a bunch of lead in me, all right?

"I was very calm . . . a normal, relaxed state. I wasn't vindictive. I wasn't mean. I wasn't angry, you know, to where I said, 'Fucking bitch,' *boom!*"

Neal said that he chose Suzanne Scott to be both a victim and his witness because she was so innocent. He knew that the other women had black marks in their past that his lawyer would have exploited at trial. He knew that Scott had no such blemishes and would make sure he paid for the crimes.

In midafternoon they took another break so that Neal could smoke. When they returned, Neal wanted to talk about Angela Fite. He wanted them to know that he never took any money from Fite. However, of the three, Angela was the only one that he was in love with, he said. That's why he promised her a home for herself and her children. "She wanted to live better. She wanted the money." He'd warned her: "You talk about the house, I'm going to kill you. You're going to die, period." When Angela betrayed his trust and told others, including her family, she had to die.

"I found out before she died that she had been running her mouth . . . about a few other things as well. And that's one of the reasons why Angie died. . . . It's like, you know, fair warning. And I said, 'Because you're a snitch, you die. I mean, I can't give you any clearer warning than that.' "

Of all the odd and self-serving things that he'd say, one of the most bizarre was that he'd talked Angie Fite into joining him as a female hit man for the mob. "She was going to have to kill somebody to prove her loyalty to me that night." He could tell by her reaction when she saw the bodies of the other women that Angela wouldn't keep her mouth shut. "She was a snitch," he said.

This was a new twist, one the investigators knew he'd never mentioned to Scott or Beth Weeks in his confessions. No one believed him now. . . . Or if she'd said it, it had been in jest, not thinking he was really a killer . . . until she saw his "mortuary."

He'd loved Angie so much, however, that he'd told her that he would kill her estranged husband, Matt Rankin. "They had a very violent relationship. I was going to do it for love: 'Nobody's going to mess with you.' " He said that he was not just going to kill Rankin, but his brother and father as well, "and if his mother was around, I'd probably have killed her, too."

Rankin had come looking for him one time at Angela Fite's apartment. Called him "a little bitch." Neal told the investigators that he normally didn't let people talk to him that way, but this time he "snuck out of the apartment so Angie wouldn't be in another domestic [violence incident].

"Matt's a piece of shit. He's violent. He's mean. They should have had him in jail for breaking the restraining order like he did. . . . She was scared to death of him. She told me

Matt Rankin was going to end up killing her."
So he was going to kill Rankin. "It was a love
thing. It was: 'I love you, baby, nobody's going
to mess with you.' "

Neal said he spread the "bounty hunter" rumor just to see where it would go, know who was
talking to whom.

"So you were never a bounty hunter, right?"
Aceves asked.

"Oh, hell no," Neal replied. "I never wanted
to be."

"You were never a hit man?"

"Never a hit man."

Neal said that he'd been bullshitting people
for so long that it had become a habit, even
when unnecessary to achieve some purpose. "I
mean, there's a book that I'm reading right now
about Bundy. It's called"—he had to think—
"shoot . . . I've read *The Stranger Beside Me*. . . .
It's not that one. . . . What's the name of that
book?" Then he remembered. *"The Only Living
Witness.*

"Bundy put it in a good way. And not that he
was an idol, but there was certain things that he
did that were close to me. He said that the more
you practice it, you were like an actor, an illusion,
that you sold somebody that you were somebody
that you weren't. That the more he practiced lying or acting the role, the better he got and the
more natural he became. It was all just an act,
playing a part.

"I don't believe that I believe my own bullshit.
That's why I had an argument with mental
health. They kept saying, 'Do you hear voices?'
No. Nobody told me to do it. I'm just a stinkin'
liar, OK?

"Candace, Rebecca, and Angie did not pay because I 'snapped.' Now, isn't that scary?"

At times when Neal was interrupted by the investigators, he irritably insisted on finishing a thought, whether or not it had to do with the question that he'd been asked. His demeanor ranged from complimenting them on their insight, to warning them not to push him into discussing subjects that he considered taboo. He even made thinly veiled threats, such as when asked about whether he felt rage.

"The rage is there," he told the investigators. "Don't fuck with me. And I don't mean that as a threat. . . . Santa Claus is coming to town, motherfucker, and you ain't going to like who shows up. You can't run, you can't hide, nothing. . . . Fuck with me and give me a reason to get out of here, and I'll find a way."

Neal turned the conversation back to Suzanne Scott. The others had betrayed him in one way or another, and so had to die, he said. Suzanne was different. "She did not deserve to have anything happen to her other than she was an innocent. She was the most innocent one that I knew that could tell them: 'This is a warning—don't fuck with me, all right? Don't open your fat mouth, OK? You better keep yourself quiet or you're going to die, all right?"

There never had been anybody else in the room upstairs, he said. The noises that they'd heard, and he'd pretended to react to, had been the neighbor walking about. However, he surprised the investigators by telling them that someone else saw Holberton's body.

"Who was that?" Aceves asked. If this was true, two murders could have been prevented. . . .

Maybe the witness could be charged with accessory to murder after the fact.

"I'll never share that," Neal said, and smiled. "He was not involved in the murder."

"But he could be a witness to what she said," Aceves countered. "When did that person see Rebecca dead?"

"The day that she died," Neal replied. "That's all I'll tell you. . . . I have a problem with snitches, sir."

"Why do you feel that this person hasn't come forth?" Aceves asked.

"Because they're not a snitch, either," Neal said, now referring to "he" as "they." "They're good people, and they've never been involved in anything wrong at all. But I can tell you, they're not somebody to fuck with, either. . . . I almost snapped his mind over it."

Neal returned to the night that he murdered Fite. She was "flipping out" when she saw the bodies. "Angie knew when she said, 'We're not going to get out of here alive, are we?' is because she knew I had her number, too. . . . Her conscience was bothering her that she had betrayed my warnings."

After Angela Fite died, Suzanne agreed with him that she couldn't be trusted. But Suzanne trusted him, he said. "I don't know if she said that I was very gentle with her. I mean, you know, her and I held hands while I was sleeping. . . . She said she wasn't really asleep, but she was sleeping because I could hear her dozing. It was very stressful for her. But I know she wanted me to stay with her.

"I wanted Suzanne to be the one that made it out alive and the one that was going to send me to the chair. I wanted a living witness, so to speak, as a warning to everybody else: Don't fuck with me; I've had enough. Time out . . . because then I'm going to lose it, and I haven't lost it up to this point."

When he left Scott, Weeks, and David Cain on the day that he surrendered, Neal said that he'd considered going back to the town house "and blowing my brains out." But when he spotted the crime scene tape, he turned away.

Aceves asked if he'd sexually assaulted or urinated on Fite.

"No, sir," he replied. "I loved Angie. I just didn't like somebody betraying me. . . . I've been betrayed since I was a little kid."

Zimmerman asked if he was bitter toward the women he'd killed. "I felt bitter in a way, but . . . I didn't use bitterness with that ax in my hand splitting her brain, OK, to execute her, right?"

Neal said that he purposely wanted the murders to be as brutal as possible. "I wanted no way out. I wanted this picture to be so horrendous that society would not let me get off—OK?—because I don't deserve to get off. Not for one murder, not for two, not for three, not for raping Suzanne."

He said that he'd been troubled by nightmares since the murders. "My conscience has always bothered me . . . and that touched me, because then I knew that I still had one. That gave me hope rather than being so cold and cruel and saying, 'Hey, fuck it, man, it's just a bunch of dead bitches.' I've cried many times in my cell after these murders.

"Hell, last night I cried for over an hour on what little I've been able to see in my mind again. . . . Rebecca's little head sitting under that blanket looking so precious . . . Candace looking so studious and trusting, as much as she could . . . The lady I really love, Angie . . . Poor little Suzanne.

"I'm able to deal with it, not because I'm insensitive or cruel or a demon or evil, I'm hanging on for the ones that died. I'm hanging on for Suzanne. I'll be all right."

Neal said that there was one thing he'd noticed about his kitten's reaction to the murders. "I loved that little kitty," he said. "But after Rebecca died, her little tummy would not come off that floor. She knew I was a killer. It was like she definitely knew that I had it in me, because cats are—what do you call them?—predators. She recognized a bigger predator.

"And that's what I was: a predator is something that stalks, calculates, is committed to a kill . . . knows when to spring or jump. That would describe me as well."

The investigators at last returned to the question of how he intended to get rid of the bodies. Did he intend to dismember his victims, place them in the footlockers, and then try to hide the evidence? Had he simply run out of steam after all the killing?

Carnivores, Neal said. He'd planned to get rid of the bodies by leaving them for wild carnivores after he had disposed of the victims' heads, hands, and feet so that they couldn't be identified. He said that he had a secret place where he'd been baiting the carnivores for years for just that purpose.

Such careful planning suggested to them that the killer was someone who knew what he was doing and possibly had done it before. "Cody, for never having killed somebody before this time, you sure had this really well planned out," Zimmerman noted.

"In a short amount of time," Neal reminded her.

"And you covered yourself every step of the way," the investigator continued.

"Yeah," he agreed, "except for leaving everything where you could get it."

"OK, so have you ever killed somebody before?" Zimmerman asked.

"No," he said. "And I'll lay that on my mother's life, OK, never."

Although he claimed that Bundy was not his idol, Neal conceded that he "related to Bundy in a lot of ways. Not because he was a mentor with me. I don't believe I really ever read a Bundy book before I was in jail, but I've heard things.

"I was better than Bundy would have ever been, OK? . . . I'm not meaning that bragging. I'm saying that I had this killer in me all my life, and I've depressed it."

He had contemplated killing "at least thirty more people I was going to get within a three-day period. I had them lined up, ready to go, and there was no doubt I could have got them all. And every one of those people I knew."

A lot of them were supposed friends at the bars that he frequented, Shipwreck's and Fugglies. "It was going to be a wipeout thing. Make sure they're all there, and go in and kill every last one of the sons of bitches who was there." He said that he'd planned an especially tortuous death for Matt Rankin and Rankin's brother and father.

Most of the later victims were just garbage anyway, he said, like Gerloff. "I was going to make a judgment call," he said, on who would live and who would die.

There was a passage in the Bible, Revelation 6:8, that he thought the investigators might want to look up. "It's about this pale horse, and on it was a rider, and his name was Death, and Hades followed him." Neal looked at his interrogators. "That's me, OK? That's me."

Fourteen

District Court Judge Thomas Woodford looked down from his bench at the defendant in the jail jumpsuit. "How do you plead?" he asked.

"Guilty," Cody Neal responded. "Without a doubt, Your Honor."

At least this time he'd told the truth and followed through on a promise. Following his arrest and through the rest of 1998, Neal had continued trying to tell his story to just about anybody who would listen, though the story often changed.

In one interview, he would be telling a newspaper reporter, "I'll plead guilty to any stinking charge they got, without a plea bargain. I want the death penalty. I believe I deserve it." And in the next, he would express his desire to remain alive in prison so that he could devote his life to teaching others about Jesus.

With members of the media, his approach was almost always the same—flattery, a promise to reveal previously unknown aspects of his crime and background, and "an exclusive." Rarely was anything new revealed as a result of these interviews, but he could usually find a taker to listen to him.

Then he would break off the interview and a week later make the same promises to another reporter.

Neal was always trying to paint himself as now dedicated to "the truth" and doing the right thing, though always with a hint that he was not alone to blame. He said he wanted to avoid a trial so that details of the victims' lives wouldn't be made public. "They didn't do nothin' wrong," he told a newspaper. "Why should it be put in the public eye? I want to get on with it. Not that I want to die. But I know it's a death penalty case. I always believed in the death penalty, myself. And I still believe in the death penalty. I do have a heart and I do have a conscience."

Talking to investigators, the press, family, and friends, he'd confessed to a variety of motives for committing the crimes. A few days after his interviews with Jose Aceves and Cheryl Zimmerman in September 1998, Neal repeated parts of the story for a newspaper columnist. He boasted about having been involved in all sorts of illegal activities: "Theft, extortion, fraud, embezzlement, forgery. I could keep listing them."

As for the women, "I knew they'd be potential snitches. I was right—none of them were trustable." Candace Walters had told Holberton about his criminal activities, he said, but he was able to "smooth things over." Walters then hinted that she'd talked to Angela Fite. "They pushed me to my limit," he said. "I don't want to say I 'snapped.' All three had fair warning."

Neal also boasted that he was a Mafia hit man doing a job. He said that he'd killed the women because he'd been worried that they were going to turn him in for bilking them of their money.

Suzanne Scott told investigators, "He wanted people to start listening to him and believing what he said." David Cain said that Neal told him that "he would get a rush out of killing people."

In jail Neal's reading revolved around the life and death of serial killer Ted Bundy, who'd been executed in Florida's electric chair. Neal said that he would prefer a firing squad to Colorado's method of execution, a lethal injection. "I want justice to be served," he said. "It won't be served if I just fall asleep.

"I'm ready. I want to do it now. While it's hot, let's eat."

Whenever he got the chance, Neal apologized to the victims' families. "I am truly sorry to have you all go through this nightmare. I will say you have a right to know why," he told a reporter, then added mysteriously, "I will do my best to answer that at a later time and place."

The families cared little about what he had to say; their loved ones had done nothing worse than care for a man who had robbed them and then murdered them. There could be no excuse. Nor was Holly Walters, for one, moved by his supposed acceptance of the death penalty. "It's not even going to be up to him," she told the press. "At this point, I don't care what Cody wants, regardless of whether it's in our favor or not. I have no feelings for Cody whatsoever, other than hate."

In November 1998, investigator Cheryl Zimmerman had testified at Neal's preliminary hearing to show cause why he was charged. She'd recounted how he'd told her that he killed his roommate, Rebecca Holberton, and then lured

Candace Walters and Angela Fite to their deaths with a promise of "a big surprise" that awaited them. As objectively as possible, the police officer had detailed how each victim was seated in the chair and then struck with the long-handled maul. After he taped Fite to the chair, she had testified, he pointed out the bodies and the presence of Suzanne Scott, then said, "Welcome to my mortuary."

A date was set at the preliminary for the arraignment, with Neal contending that he would plead guilty at that time. But his public defender, Jim Aber, sounded like he was mounting a defense when he asked Zimmerman on cross-examination, "Why would he commit murder to avoid being charged with theft?"

By the time the arraignment rolled around in February 1999, Aber was gone. Neal had fired him after an argument over his decision to plead guilty. Reluctantly, he'd accepted Randy Canney, a former public defender who was now in private practice, as an advisory counsel. Neal now conceded that he was going against Canney's advice. However, he noted to the court, he'd recently met with a psychiatrist "who didn't see any reason why I was not competent."

As Neal spoke, Canney sat quietly at the defense table. He believed that his client was mentally ill and delusional; he had hoped that the psychiatric examination would have found him incompetent to proceed with a trial. But the hurdle for competence was low; Neal had to be so sick as to not understand the nature of the charges or the penalties that he would face if convicted. He understood both. There was little the lawyer could do now to prevent the defendant from essentially committing suicide.

Several times, Judge Woodford asked Neal if he wanted to reconsider his plea and have a lawyer appointed to represent him. Each time Neal refused.

"This is the point of no return," Woodford finally warned him.

"I understand that, sir," he replied.

Woodford shrugged and accepted Neal's plea. There was only one last thing to do: set a date for Neal's death penalty hearing. Only then did the defendant imply that he was going to put up a fight.

Normally, a hearing would have been held within sixty days, but Neal asked Woodford to extend the time so he could do research in the jail's law library. He also asked for permission to spend at least twelve hours a week doing the research. The judge granted both requests and set the hearing date for July.

As Neal was being led from the courtroom, a young man sitting with the victims' families yelled, "Hey, punk! Hey, punk!" Neal didn't turn or acknowledge that he'd heard as family members and victims' advocate counselors settled the young man down.

After that hearing, Neal's former attorney, Jim Aber, criticized Jefferson County District Attorney Dave Thomas for continuing to seek the death penalty. "This is a total farce," he told the press after Neal's guilty plea. "Seeking the death penalty against a person not represented by counsel is like trying to kill an unarmed man. There is no morality or justice in this."

Thomas shrugged off Aber's accusation, at

least in the press. "The death penalty motion in this case is appropriate," he said. "Our job as prosecutor is to pursue justice as we see fit."

However, the prosecutors who would be trying the case—Chief Deputy District Attorney Charles Tingle, who'd been in on the crime scene investigation, and Deputy District Attorney Chris Bachmeyer—considered Aber's comments a cheap shot.

By Aber's logic, all a murder defendant would have to do to avoid the possibility of a death sentence would be to demand to represent himself, *pro se* in the latin legalese. Then the prosecution would be morally obligated not to seek the death penalty.

They saw the comment as political grandstanding; in actuality, the prosecution would have preferred that Neal be represented by counsel. They had what they believed to be an overwhelming case. The only real question was Neal's competency, but the defendant had repeatedly said that he knew that murdering the women and raping Scott was wrong—the hurdle for legal insanity—and had been deemed competent to proceed at trial by the psychiatrist.

Thomas even said that he would have preferred for Neal to have a lawyer. By representing himself, Neal guaranteed that if sentenced to die, appellate lawyers would argue during the appeals stage that he had not been competent to represent himself. It would be one more issue that the Colorado Attorney General's Office, which handled such appeals for district attorneys, would have to deal with. If an appellate court agreed with those assertions, then Jefferson County would have to go through the death penalty hearing, possibly an entire trial, again.

At the district attorney's office, they talked about whether that was all part of Neal's plan. Nothing seemed beyond his cunning.

For the next seven months, Charles Tingle and Chris Bachmeyer proceeded with extra care. Cody Neal would have to be afforded rights and privileges that the usual defendant did not receive. It had already been an exhausting case, and even more drawn out when Neal asked for another extension and was given until September.

Tingle had the most contact with Neal, including Canney, except, perhaps, investigator Aceves. As a *pro se* defendant, Neal had the right to contact Tingle to discuss legal matters, as would any attorney appointed to represent him. Neal took full advantage of phone privileges granted by the judge, calling the prosecutor four or five times a week, leaving messages when no one was in.

Although he was not allowed to tape their other conversations, Tingle could and did keep the voice-mail messages; since the arraignment, he'd accumulated two hours of Neal's ramblings, at an average of a minute a message. It wasn't unusual to come to the office on Monday morning and find ten messages or more from the defendant, who would talk until cut off by the machine, then call back, often only to repeat the same information.

Forty years old, dark-haired, and brown-eyed, Charles Tingle looked like a district attorney—conservative, straitlaced, white shirts and plain

ties, clean-cut. In fifteen years as a prosecutor, he'd
never run into anybody like Cody Neal. The defendant was extremely intelligent, at least in his
niche as a pathological liar and sociopath. He was
also very meticulous, putting together an eigh-
teen-inch-thick stack of case law regarding the
death penalty in the United States. It was clear
from their conversations that he'd read every page
of it, as well as the thousands and thousands of
pages of discovery. If there was a page that he
couldn't read or a clarification that he needed,
he'd stay after Tingle until he got what he wanted,
rather than let it slip like most *pro se* defendants
that the prosecutor had dealt with in the past
would do.

Given the methodical way that Neal had gone
about the business of murdering three women
and raping a fourth, it wasn't really a surprise.
If there was one thing that stood out about the
murders, beyond their brutality, it was the incredible, multilayered web of lies and details that
he'd spun to snare his victims. Even when the
tales had grown past the point of credulity to
anyone looking at this case from the outside, it
was a reflection of his ability as a "master manipulator" that he was able to lead the women
so easily into his lair.

It was one of Tingle's fears that Neal would be
underestimated. By the courts. By his jailers. By
even himself and Bachmeyer. He adopted the attitude that anything, no matter how innocent,
that came out of the defendant's mouth was an
attempt to manipulate them.

In their pretrial dealings, Neal was always cour-
teous and respectful . . . ingratiatingly so. Although he would become irritated if some issue

had not been taken care of fast enough to suit him, he was never threatening on the telephone or in the dozen face-to-face meetings that they had. Only on one occasion did he ask if Tingle, who always took an investigator as both a witness and for safety's sake, was too nervous to meet with him alone.

Otherwise, Neal was always handing out compliments about how honorable and smart he was. He couldn't thank the prosecutors, both Tingle and Bachmeyer, enough for respecting him and helping him pursue the *pro se* course that he was on.

It made Tingle's skin crawl to hear him talk like they were on the same team. He knew from firsthand experience what Neal had done; he'd been called to the scene while the bodies were still there, had seen the blood pooled on the floor and splattered on the wall with brain matter. The vision of what he'd seen had haunted him ever since. He'd prosecuted more than a dozen murder cases, all with their own crime scene and autopsy photographs, but none had come close to what he'd had to study to prepare for this case.

To even be able to look at Neal without revulsion, he had to separate in his mind the ax-murderer from the jailhouse lawyer. But even after all that he had done, and facing the death penalty, Neal had not changed his ways. Haircuts in the jail cost $6, and Tingle had seen records that showed Neal paying with $20, leaving a $14 tip. He was apparently receiving money from friends, including a new girlfriend.

Even inside the jail, Neal was still the dream-weaver. Whatever a woman wanted most—

whether it was a home, financial security, adventure . . . or love—he was the one who promised to make it come true. He knew what buttons to push, which strings to pull.

Fifteen

July 28, 1999, Jefferson County Detention Center

William Lee Neal walked into the interview room with a grin on his face and his hand extended. "I'm Cody Neal," he said, shaking hands with this writer like a used-car salesman, warm and ingratiating. "Cody's a nickname. . . . My friends call me Cody."

He glanced to the left, then smiled and exchanged nods with another inmate through the glass partition separating the tiny room from the cubicle next door. "He's a great guy . . . brings me my food every morning," Neal said of the younger man, who had been laughing wildly at whatever his weepy mother was telling him through the thick Plexiglas that separated her from her son.

There was no such barrier in this room. Neal demanded a contact visit to tell his story because, he said, he didn't want "other people" to hear. The request was at first denied by jail authorities; he was, after all, a confessed mass murderer. When he complained to jail higher-ups, the request was quickly granted—"Whatever Cody wants"—so long as he behaved himself and there

were no delays getting to his death penalty trial
in September.

There had been a number of "special considerations" that he'd been given by the district attorney's and sheriff's offices due to his choice to
represent himself. *Pro se* defendants were allowed
a certain number of hours in the jail's law library
to prepare their defense. In Neal's case, the jail
brought in extra personnel so that he could
spend entire nights in the library, sometimes with
a fellow inmate hired to help him make copies
and collate his material. The court ordered that
a tape recorder be purchased for him so that he
could listen to taped interviews and make dupli-
cates (as well as pass the time listening to his
music). He had a VCR and television so that he
could watch videos, such as those of his confessions; he was allowed to keep law books, legal
materials, and all sorts of writing materials—provided by the court—in his cell.

He even had a cell phone, which he was allowed to call out on for a total of one hour a
day, including long distance. He'd entered a motion saying that he had a lot of people—friends
and family—out of state that he might need to
summon as witnesses. The phone was supposed
to be so that he could prepare his defense, but
he used it for a variety of reasons, including calling a new girlfriend in Arizona, and contacting
the press. He'd run up monthly telephone bills,
including one for nearly $1,000, talking on a
daily basis to the one sibling in his family who
would speak to him, his sister Sharon.

In the interview room, he leaned forward con-
spiratorially and said in a stage whisper that he
did his best to use the phone on the Q.T. "I

don't want these other inmates trying to take advantage of the folks here at the jail, who've been real good to me." But ten minutes per call wasn't enough, he complained, so he planned to petition the court for more airtime.

Manipulating, always manipulating—that's Wild Bill Cody Neal, the forty-three-year-old charismatic killer who threw money around on strippers, limos, and parties like it was sand at the beach. He took a seat on one of the two plain stools that rose out of the floor like gray mushrooms; between them an equally drab and secured table jutted from the wall. Mass murderer or not, he didn't look dangerous. His blue eyes were a bit too pale and widely spaced on his round face—and therefore somewhat disconcerting, but really only if the viewer was aware of what he did.

Otherwise, he was rather unmenacing, five-foot-eight and a bit pear-shaped, with short, undefined arms and soft, damp hands. His thick brown hair perched uncombed on top of his head like an unkempt cat. He now had the pallor of a corpse—he didn't want much recreation time and avoided most opportunities to socialize with other inmates. The skin around his eyes was puffy, as if he weren't sleeping well with his death penalty hearing looming. The muted light of the single fluorescent tube in the ceiling of the interview room and the gray cinder-block walls and blue-tinged institutional carpeting did little to improve his complexion. Only the bright orange jail jumpsuit that he wore and his voice—a gravelly baritone with a western rumble that one might expect from an old cowboy—gave him any color or substance.

Neal began by saying how he wanted to tell his story and to keep telling it along the road to his expected execution. But some parts, he confided, needed to be kept quiet for the time being. He said that he didn't want his court-appointed advisory counsel, Randy Canney, to use his story to try to save his life, or the prosecution in its efforts to kill him. So he hadn't told any of them much about his life, he confided, and would now have to be careful how much he revealed. "There's family members who's ill or don't know the situation I'm in, and I don't want them contacted or subpoenaed."

With that he was ready to talk. His modus operandi with the press was to call, flatter—"I've read your stuff, and you're the only reporter in this town who can do this justice"—say what he hoped would find its way into a newspaper or television report, then move on to the next reporter: "I've read your stuff, and you're the only reporter in this town who can do this justice." He always claimed to have something "new," something to add, but it was always the same old story. . . . Always something to do with how he was struggling mightily to represent himself in court, against all legal advice, so that "the truth" would come out and his victims and their families would be spared further pain. . . . Always as though there were some sort of nobility to his "sacrifice."

The truth, he complained, was being "twisted by lies in the press." Inaccuracies about what he did that—"bad as it was"—were "sensationalized," especially in regard to Suzanne Scott. "They said I made her watch," he whined as he had to sheriff's investigators Jose Aceves and

Cheryl Zimmerman in September 1998. "In fact, I told her not to. . . . I told her to turn her head so she couldn't see. . . . But after she heard the sound from the first time I hit Angie, she looked and saw the rest."

Considering the circumstances, he said, he behaved like a gentleman when he sexually assaulted her. "Rape is rape," he conceded. "But she even told the detectives that I was real gentle with her."

Despite the carnage and sorrow that he had caused, Neal saw himself as "owning up." It's why, he said, he pleaded guilty in February to three counts of first-degree murder, three counts of sexual assault, and seven other counts that included felony menacing and kidnapping.

"We need to end the violence by taking responsibility for our actions," he said. "But as some old Turk once said, 'No matter how long you've gone down the wrong road, turn back, turn back.' "

Part of his turning back, he said, was to "protect the good names" of the women he'd butchered. But at the same time, he hinted—as he had to the investigators—that there were aspects of his victims' lives that his attorney could exploit. "My counsel's saying I'm hurtin' the families more not goin' to trial 'cause there's no closure for 'em. . . . But they'll get their justice in the penalty phase. I still say I deserve to die for what I done, and I can't see puttin' 'em through more'n what they been through already."

Neal quickly added, however, that the people who contended that he was representing himself because he wanted to die had it wrong. "I want to live and contribute," he said, admitting that it had also crossed his mind that "owning up" might persuade the panel of three judges who would hear his case to spare his life. "It's my only chance."

Right now, he said, he was having difficulty with Canney. "He wants me to reverse my guilty plea and is threatening to petition the court that I'm not competent to represent myself."

He sighed. It was exhausting trying to do the right thing. "I'm fightin' more with my defense counsel than the prosecution," he noted. "I get along real well with Tingle. He's been helpin' me protect my rights to self-representation and to accept responsibility by pleadin' guilty. And I'm thankful for that." As if part of a team headed to the Super Bowl, rather than a man whom the prosecution would like strapped to a steel table and given a lethal injection, he said that he was "workin' hard" with the prosecutors and jail authorities to "avoid any sort of snags."

On the other hand, he conceded, Canney didn't think that he was prepared for the hearing, "and that could be true." There were some ten thousand pages of discovery to read—including the transcript of the seven-and-a-half-hour confession that he gave Aceves and Zimmerman. He complained that he still hadn't received some of the addresses and telephone numbers that he needed to implement his "strategy" (which he wouldn't reveal) for the hearing.

With all that said, he turned to what he claimed one of his jailers told him was " 'an extraordinary life . . . from livin' with the rich and famous . . . to the dregs . . . and through all kinds of employment.' " Not even his family knew his tale, he said. "I've lived a private life . . . where I didn't want them involved in it."

At his death penalty hearing in September 1999, Neal knew he would be asked to present "mitigators"—reasons countering the prosecution's arguments, called "aggravators," that he should be put to death. In many death penalty trials, mitigators include tales of physical, emotional, and sexual abuse in childhood, or addictions to drugs and alcohol that left the defendant unable to assess the impact of his behavior, or a lack of criminal history, or even past good deeds that might show the defendant wasn't *all bad*.

Neal said that he'd have few, if any, such mitigators. "I grew up in an all-American family." His father was "a good man, a disciplinarian. . . . It was 'Yes, ma'am,' and 'No, sir,' and 'Don't you raise your voice to your mother,' or you'd find your lip on the wall." His father was also a very honest man who taught his two sons and two daughters the difference between right and wrong. "Don't steal. Don't lie. Do what's right, tell the truth. . . . And if you do something wrong, 'You better come to me before somebody else does.' "

Despite the lectures, Neal said, he was a boy when he got his first taste of the sort of petty crimes that would accelerate in his adult life. He was ten years old when he and a friend were caught shoplifting toy cars at a local five-and-dime by the woman who owned the store. Brought to her office, where a security guard loomed over them menacingly, the woman threatened to call their fathers. "I was cryin' and beggin', 'No, anything but that,' " he said with a laugh.

He and his friend talked their way out of trouble, promising that they'd never steal again. "She thought she was givin' me a break," he said. "And we thought we had really put one over on her. . . . But she should have called my dad and had him whip the tar out of me. . . . Maybe if she didn't give me a break, things woulda been different."

Still, it wasn't like he suddenly "went bad." He didn't start committing other crimes until he was an older teenager, he said. Nor was he rebelling against his parents. He said how he was proud that his father was a decorated World War II veteran, a radio operator in a bomber who flew missions all over the South Pacific. "He won the Distinguished Flying Cross. If it looked like it was going to be a bad run, he'd fly for the married guys with kids."

Neal said that he got his "passion" for country music from his dad. "You know, Hank Williams Sr., Johnny Cash." There was even a little Rick Nelson from 1961. . . . " 'Hello Mary Lou, Goodbye heart,' " he sang, breaking out in an impromptu serenade. He wasn't sure but believed that his dad retired from the service "when I was nine or so.

"Some of these dates are hard to pin down," he said. "I have a lot of places where the memory just isn't there." After retirement the old man's alcoholism got worse, and he was quicker to lay it on his son's backside with a leather belt. But it wasn't the occasional beatings that his son minded so much as the efforts to embarrass him in front of the other drunks at the bars that he'd drag young Bill to: "He'd think it was funny. Then he'd black out and forget all about it."

For comfort Neal turned to his mother. "I absolutely loved my mother." The mention of her and a glance at the mother talking to her son in the next room brought tears to his eyes and his voice grew even huskier as he tried to describe her. "Mom was awesome," he said. "The definition of love was my mom.

"She was beautiful, a gorgeous brunette. She looked like a movie star. But she was very much the mother . . . devoted to her family."

Neal said that his parents never fought. One word from his soft-spoken mother was enough to let his dad know he had stepped over the line. "And he would do anything to make it right."

It would be better for him, Neal acknowledged, if there was some dark secret—some evil done to him by his father, or some twisted relationship with his mother—that caused a brooding anger that might explain to the panel of judges why he did what he did in June and July of 1998. But no, he said, there was nothing there.

"So what if I got beat when I did something wrong, 'Spare the rod, spoil the child,' " he said, but added that there was something that "turned out the light" of an active, friendly boy.

Neal said that as a child he'd known what he wanted to be when he grew up, or at least had a couple of ideas; neither of them included being an ax-murderer. One possibility was becoming an FBI agent; his father had taken him to the agency's headquarters in Washington, D.C., and he looked through the museum with its histories of Eliot Ness and J. Edgar Hoover. A G-man sounded like a fun and exciting career, and he could do a lot of good, catching bad guys and all.

His other choice was to be a minister. He'd been named after a family pastor, William Lee. One of his uncles was also a minister. "He was kind and gentle . . . and he helped people who were hurtin'. I loved The Word and Lord Jesus, and I liked going to Sunday school 'cause people just seem to be nicer on Sunday."

Neal paused, furrowed his brow, and growled, "Never did like mean people. . . . My sister told me there was a bad storm when I was born, and that was the reason there was a light about me. I always got along with everybody and loved people." When he was twelve or thirteen years old, he said, the light was extinguished. An older, married woman invited him to apply lotion to her legs, "and it went from there." The woman's husband was running around on her, he said, so she was using him as a way to get even. The guilt was enormous.

"I couldn't wash myself enough," he said. Nor could he talk to anybody about what was going on. "She said if I ever told, my family would disown me." On the other hand, sex with a beautiful woman wasn't all bad. "It was such a contradiction. I enjoyed it, but afterward I would feel so guilty."

In the interview room, Neal rubbed his palms together. "It was like the two sides in me was sanding each other, and there wasn't much left in between." The affair continued for about six months, during which time he turned the tables and began molesting a young girl.

The older woman was the one who finally called the affair off. They never talked about it again until he got out of the army, which he had joined shortly after his seventeenth birthday in

October 1972. The woman was divorced by this time and, he said, eager to resume their affair. "I told her, 'You had me as a boy; now have me as a man.'" When he was ready to leave, he said, she was talking about staying together, even marrying. "But that's where it ended. I turned and walked away.

"I have no ill feelings towards her. Lord knows what she's goin' through now, wonderin' if she was the cause of all of this. She was just passin' on her anger and pain, almost like it was a demon, and givin' it to me. I don't blame her, but that's when the light went out.

"I became more distant from my family, not as cheerful. I started gettin' into trouble more. I knew I couldn't be a minister or an FBI agent . . . not after what I done."

There are other claims of sexual abuse in which he was the "unwilling victim"—once by a church elder while in his teens and once by an army sergeant.

In September 1998, when Neal sat down with investigators Aceves and Zimmerman, he complained plenty about the women in his life—from the married woman, to his four wives, to his four victims in June and July of 1998. But, he said, he didn't want it to sound like he was blaming his rampage on others. . . . Except, he said, there was one thing that females did to him that he still resented. When they were all kids, his sisters used to lie and say that he hurt them to get him in trouble, he complained. "They'd make up stories that I hit or choked them. They'd even do things like squeeze their arms or necks and then say, 'Look what Bill did.'

"Then Dad would beat the tar out of me with

his belt while my sisters would peek in at what was goin' on and laugh. I'm not sayin' I never did any of that . . . but ninety percent of what they said I did wasn't true. . . . Just like what people are sayin' about me now, a lot of it ain't true."

Years later, with their mother dying of cancer, he said, his sisters confessed how they'd framed him. "My mother was furious with them for getting me beat for something I didn't do." His eyes welled up again at the thought of his mother on her deathbed.

Suddenly the young man in the cubicle next door threw his head back and shrieked with laughter as his poor mother wiped at her eyes and tried to smile. Neal paused in midsentence; his mouth hung open and a scowl creased his face. He looked at his breakfast waiter and shook his head as if he couldn't believe that he had to live with people who acted . . . well, so damned crazy.

"It's like going to bed one night," he said quietly, "and waking up in the pit."

Sixteen

September 20, 1999

William Lee "Cody" Neal shuffled into the Jefferson County courtroom in the standard-issue Halloween-orange jumpsuit, white T-shirt and socks, and blue slippers. Hunched over as he waited for the deputy to unlock the handcuffs behind him, he risked a quick glance back at the spectator gallery.

If looks could kill, he would have crumpled immediately to the floor of the courtroom. The families and friends of his victims, who'd been seated first, filled the three rows of pews in the gallery behind the prosecution table and spilled over to the other side. Their eyes bored into Neal; jaws clenched and voices muttered angrily. The one victim who survived his rampage, Suzanne Scott, leaned against the shoulder of her mother.

There was not enough room in the courtroom for all the rest who wanted to get inside. However, few were there for Neal. The first row on the defense side was kept empty by the deputies in charge of court security—as much for his safety as anything else. The second row was reserved for his family, of which none were present, as well as those few supporters he had, such as Jim Aber, the public defender and staunch death penalty opponent Neal had fired.

One of Neal's supporters was Byron Plumley, a representative of the anti-death-penalty American Friends Society and adjunct professor of religious studies at Regis University in Denver. Also present was a thin, middle-aged woman dressed in black who claimed that her sister used to date Neal and that she herself was "like a sister to him." Next to her was a short, heavyset woman with crosses for earrings; she'd met him at Shipwreck's.

In the far corner of the back row—most of which was occupied by members of the press, as well as courthouse personnel who managed to squeeze in for opening statements—was a pretty, petite young woman who nestled against a thin, young man. Jennifer, the defendant's fourth wife, had appeared on television newscasts following his arrest in July 1998, apologizing on behalf of herself and his family for her former husband's atrocities. She had avoided the press after that but now felt that she needed to see and hear what had become of Wild Bill Cody, the man who had swept her off her feet and then made her life hell.

The escorting deputies released the handcuffs from behind Neal's back, and reattached them to a belly chain at the front. He sat down next to his advisory counsel, Randy Canney, and began rearranging the items in front of him: dictionary, yellow legal notepads, pens—which he arranged into a neat row—and a monitor for viewing the photographs that the prosecution would be entering into evidence. He wasn't seated long before the bailiff called those in the courtroom to their feet as the three judges—Thomas Woodford, the presiding judge from Jefferson County, and Frank Martinez and William Meyer, both from Denver—entered and took their seats on an enlarged dais built five months earlier.

The dais had been constructed especially for death penalty hearings at the Jefferson County Courthouse. In 1995 the Colorado legislature had changed the state's death penalty statute to remove the decision from the shoulders of jurors and place it onto those of a panel of three judges: the presiding judge from the trial and two selected at random by a computer from adjoining districts. The law had gone into effect in 1996, but the first test case had been the Robert Riggan hearing in April 1999, also in Jefferson County. That panel had spared Riggan, who had been accused of murdering a twenty-one-year-old prostitute in May 1997, because the jury had convicted him of murder, but not premeditated murder.

Few in the courtroom expected Neal to receive a similar judgment. Two days before the death penalty trial, Canney had attempted one last time to raise the issue of competency. The lawyer even called Neal's sister, Sharon, the one family member still talking to him, who over a speakerphone testified that her brother would go "from being rational to incoherent in the same conversation" and that he talked about being "a prophet of God." Her brother, she said, once even claimed to have been "possessed."

The lawyers were, of course, arguing "competency" as it is meant in a legal sense. What might seem like a "crazy," or insane, act—to the general public such as butchering three innocent women—does not in itself make a defendant mentally incompetent to stand trial. For a defendant to be deemed legally insane, a psychiatrist must show that the defendant didn't know right from wrong at the time of his crime, and/or the defendant is not psychologically able to understand the charges against him or assist in his defense. Woodford noted that Neal had shown no signs of mental disease in any of his multiple court appearances, and the psychiatrists had determined that Neal understood what he had done and its ramifications. The hearing would proceed.

Now at Woodford's invitation, Chief Deputy District Attorney Charles Tingle rose to deliver the prosecution's opening statements. At the table behind him were Deputy District Attorney Chris Bachmeyer and the lead investigator in the case, Jose Aceves.

Tingle had noticed something different about Neal when the defendant sat down a few minutes earlier: the killer and rapist was wearing a new gold wedding band.

It wasn't a complete surprise, a few days before the hearing he'd received a call from the deputies at the jail. An upscale Denver jewelry-store manager was complaining to them that he was getting harassing telephone calls from Neal. The defendant wanted to purchase a wedding set and felt that he was getting the runaround. Even knowing what Neal was capable of, the revelation of his impending "marriage" had come as a shock. Tingle was aware that Neal had a new girlfriend, a wealthy "trust fund baby" from Phoenix, Arizona, named Julia. They knew from his jail accounts that she sent him money regularly and had even been up to visit a number of times. According to one of their investigators, Julia said that she'd met Neal in 1995 at Fugglies, one of his bar hangouts.

Incredible, Tingle had thought, Neal was still able to cast his spells from inside a jail. Ted Bundy, the serial killer who was executed in 1989 and whose exploits had become favored reading material for Neal, had married while on death row. At least there, the woman was able to convince herself that he was innocent. There were no such doubts with Neal, who'd told anyone who'd listen that he'd killed the women.

Tingle wondered if the "wedding" was another ploy by Neal to manipulate the judges, as well as keep some poor woman on the line to supply him with money for his needs in jail and prison.

Walking to the lectern in front of the prosecution table, Tingle paused to look one more time at his notes. Preparing for the hearing, he'd worried about making a mistake that might cause the judges to spare Neal. He and Bachmeyer talked about how to approach arguing a case in front of a panel of judges as opposed to a jury. Judges were not going to be impressed by courtroom theatrics; they agreed that they were going to have to walk a fine line between presenting "just the facts" and still imparting the enormous suffering that Neal had caused. They were also going to have to be careful to avoid looking like they were taking advantage of a *pro se* defendant.

Tingle's own feelings toward Neal were of anger and outrage, but he knew that he had to temper that passion. "Rebecca Holberton, Candace Walters, and Angela Fite were all vulnerable in one way or another," he began in the hushed courtroom, "and in search of happiness, and he preyed upon each one of them.

"He promised to rescue them emotionally and financially. But he was a phony. A master manipulator . . . and he sucked them in with his lies and deceit."

Neal didn't have a job in July 1998, Tingle told the panel of judges. He hung out at neighborhood bars and strip joints. Yet he threw money around "like it was going out of style. He'd buy a ten-dollar lunch and leave a one hundred fifty percent tip. . . . The problem was, it was not his money." He had bilked Rebecca Holberton of as much as $70,000 and Candace Walters of another $6,000.

However, in the weeks and days leading up to the murders, "the walls were caving in" on Neal, the prosecutor said. Holberton, a forty-four-year-old blonde who worked at US West, was unhappy and broke. She had told a friend that she was ready to get on with her life, without Neal. But first, she wanted her money back.

Meanwhile, Walters was trying to find out more about the secretive Cody, who said that he had homes in Las Vegas and Denver, but wouldn't tell her where he lived. She had made him sign a promissory note for the money that he owed her and was threatening to expose him to Holberton and the police.

"Rather than risk being exposed for who he really was," Tingle said, "Neal came up with a plan." A week or so later, he implemented it.

In the early morning of June 30, 1998, Neal drove to Builder's Square "for a little shopping."

He bought Lava soap, four eyebolts, nylon rope, duct tape and . . . Tingle went over to the jury box in front of the prosecution table and picked up . . ."a seven-and-a-half-pound splitting maul."

Even some of the spectators who knew how the murders were accomplished groaned at the sight of the maul. But it was not *the* murder weapon. Just a facsimile. The real weapon, still stained with blood, waited for the judges' later inspection in a clear plastic bag.

By the time Neal left Builder's Square, Tingle said, placing the maul back, the defendant had "all the tools he needed to inflict immense pain, suffering, anguish, and death." He returned home and placed a chair in the middle of the living room. Calling Holberton into the room, he invited her to take a seat. He had talked about "a surprise" that he had for her, and she was, in Neal's own words, Tingle said, "filled with joy and happiness." He opened a bottle of champagne, placed a briefcase on her lap, and then covered her with a blanket to await her surprise.

Neal fetched his splitting maul and "ambushed Rebecca from behind, unleashing a violent and ferocious attack using the hammer side of the maul," Tingle said. He brought the weapon down "with such force that it completely caved in the back of her skull," sending skull fragments into her brain and a two-inch piece of bone flying across the room. Her hands came up on the first blow and were injured when caught by the second blow. The coroner, Tingle said, had been unable to ascertain exactly how many times she had been struck because of the extent of the injuries, but "it was multiple times" with both the blunt and sharp sides of the maul.

Holberton fell to the ground, "never to rise again." Neal wrapped her head in clear plastic to catch the blood and then, after binding her limbs and body with nylon rope, wrapped her in black plastic and placed her against a wall of the apartment.

From his seat at the defense table, Neal looked quickly behind to see the audience's reaction, but just as quickly ducked his head away from the hard stares. He returned his attention to Tingle and took notes on the yellow legal pad.

The day after killing Holberton, Tingle continued, Neal told Walters about a trust fund worth millions that had finally been unfrozen upon his just settled divorce. Walters, who half believed that he was a onetime hit man for the Mafia, was informed that she would now be "paid handsomely for maintaining her silence" regarding some of the stories that he'd told her. Tingle explained to the judges how the amount had changed radically in the weeks and days before her murder. One hundred thousand dollars. A million. Two-and-a-half million. "There would also be a new home, a mansion really, down the street from his own mansion in Las Vegas."

Neal was the consummate liar. So good he persuaded her to sell her car, in anticipation of a new one, and asked her to look into what it would take to have a large amount of money wired into her account. On July 3, Tingle noted, Walters saw her daughter, Holly, "for what would be the last time." Holly Walters had her own concerns about Neal, he said, but it had been a long time since she had seen her mother so happy, so she let her misgivings slide and went on her trip to Missouri.

The next day, Neal took Walters to the town house on West Chenango Drive. She, too, sat happily in the chair, wearing a white sundress, waiting for her "surprise." But she wouldn't accept being covered with a blanket "because she didn't want her hair messed up."

Neal disappeared from her sight, Tingle said. When he returned, he was once again carrying the maul, "which he brought crashing down on the back of her head with a tremendous impact." This time, however, he used the blade side of the maul and struck four times.

"Candace Walters died a horrible, violent death," Tingle said. "For what? . . . Unarmed, defenseless . . . hoping for a better future and life." Candace's death, however, wasn't enough. He "denigrated and abused her corpse. . . . He couldn't leave her in peace, even in death, and urinated on her head and shoulders as she lay in a pool of her own blood . . . an ultimate act of debasement and disrespect for human dignity." He then wrapped her head in white plastic, and he moved her body to the ground "and covered her with a blanket so she could not be easily observed."

The defendant, Tingle noted, had killed two women in four days, "but that did not satiate his appetite. . . . It was far from over." He took Holberton's and Walters's credit cards and withdrew money from their bank accounts. "It was time to party and have a good time."

The prosecutor described the night on the town Neal enjoyed with Beth Weeks and Suzanne Scott. Before Tingle finished his account, another young woman, Angela Fite, was dead, and Scott, who sat in the spectator gallery crying quietly on her

mother's shoulder, had been raped and terrorized.

The people would be proving six "aggravating
factors," the prosecutor told the judges. Whatever mitigation the defense offered to counter
the weight of the prosecution's case, he added,
would "pale in comparison."

Looking first at Neal, Tingle then turned back
to the judges and said that it was his hope that
the court would "look at the horror of this murder, the brutal contempt for human life" and
render the only appropriate punishment.

"Death."

After Charles Tingle took his seat, Judge
Woodford called upon the defendant to make his
opening statement. With a sigh, Neal stood and
walked over to the lectern. The freedom to move
across the courtroom without leg shackles was
part of the deal that he'd worked out so that he
would be free to play the role of a lawyer. The
deputies took a couple of steps closer just in case.

As with most defendants who appear in today's
courtrooms, Neal had been offered the opportunity to dress in civilian clothes. Defense lawyers
contend that jail garb can influence judges and
jurors against their clients. Neal had turned
down the offer, saying he only deserved to wear
his inmate jumpsuit.

Before he could begin, Woodford warned him:
while opening statements are not considered evidence at any trial—just an outline of what each
side intends to present—the judge noted that
whatever Neal said about the crimes could still be
used against him and that he retained his right to

remain silent. Neal said that he understood but
wanted to go on. He adjusted the microphone at
the lectern and begged the judges' pardon if he
spoke too loud. Then he began.

"It's September 20, 1999, Monday morning, a
day that's much more to some, much less to others." As those in the courtroom probably were
aware, he said, it was Yom Kippur, "a special
day . . . the day of atonement, a day for reconciliation, forgiveness, and peace."

The faces of the families behind him were un-
moved. "This is one of the most horrendous
things I ever heard of," Neal continued, as if talking about an act committed by another man.
Then he acknowledged: "How could someone
do what I have done? I wish I could say I was
innocent. There is no excuse for this crime. I
can't wash my hands enough for this."

Neal said he was guilty as charged. "Mr. Tingle
is an honorable man and he speaks the truth. He
has been honest with me, and did not exaggerate
anything. I would not change what he said, except
maybe to fill in some blanks." And by doing so, he
said, he would be "the voice for three wonderful,
trusting, beautiful women."

Neal launched into his oft-repeated spiel about
the truth setting him free. He had been molested
as a boy, he noted, "an excuse" that led him to
spend his life "pointing the blame at someone else
while refusing to look at myself."

The weight of his deeds would be too much
to carry, he said, except for his recently reaf-
firmed "belief in the Lord, my God." Until then,
he had "served only Satan. . . . I'm not bragging; I'm so ashamed."

On his behalf, he reminded the judges that he

had fired his public defenders so that in their "zeal" to defend him, they would not further injure the victims or their families. He now promised he wouldn't cross-examine his rape victim or other prosecution witnesses. But he reserved the right to "leave open" whether he would take the stand to testify on his own behalf.

There was an old Turkish proverb, he told the judges: "No matter how long you've gone down the wrong road, turn back, turn back." He'd turned back, he said. "Even a wretched life means something. Even a wretched life can change. I do not want to die, for I know I've turned around." He wanted to live so that he could "zealously" serve Jesus in prison. And, though he did not explain how it would be accomplished, he promised "full restitution." However, if the judges decided on death, he added, "I will submit fully" to that fate, "remembering special moments" with his victims.

Neal rambled on for the better part of the morning. At one point, he acknowledged "the evil" of killing Angela Fite, "knowing how close she was as a mother to her children." Saying the word "mother" caused his voice to crack and he wiped at his cheek.

"I know better than to expect something good to come out of this," he said. But he hoped that the hearing would bring "reconciliation and forgiveness."

Because he was facing the judges, Neal did not see the families when they shook their heads back and forth. No. There would be no forgiveness from them for William Lee "Cody" Neal.

Neal moved on, saying he must always "be on guard against the evil coming back." He reminded the judges that he had never killed before, never raped a woman.

In his opening, Tingle didn't specify the aggravators—those particular, legally mandated circumstances that set apart a death penalty case from another murder—that the state would seek to prove, but Neal did it for him. The crime was "especially heinous, cruel, and depraved," he said, adding, "That's an accurate assessment." He killed two or more people by lying in wait. "True." He intentionally killed two or more people with "universal malice and extreme indifference to the value of human life. . . . True." He killed a kidnapped person. "True." He killed to prevent prosecution. "That's what precipitated the whole thing." And he killed for monetary gain. "Yes," he concluded, "all of the aggravating factors are present."

As for mitigators that might sway the judges toward life in prison, Neal said, there were only three. He surprised those in the courtroom by claiming one mitigator was "the age of the defendant," a mitigator usually reserved for very young offenders. Although he was forty-two at the time of the crime, Neal explained, being the victim of sexual abuse at an early age had left him "a child . . . hiding and stalking . . . scared of being punished for what he had been doing and what he had become."

Another mitigator, he said, was that he might not have been in the frame of mind to "appreciate the wrongfulness of his conduct." Then again, he admitted, "I knew that what I was going to do was wrong and chose to do it anyway." He only halfheartedly offered that he might have been under "unusual and substantial duress. . . .

I been through a lot of tough times in my life."
What he had become, Neal said, did not "happen overnight. . . . It took time to build a box
to live in and hide. There's no light in that box,
just the presence of evil and evil cannot stand
the light."

No mitigation could morally justify his crimes,
he said. "How can you justify the murder of
three women and the rape of a twenty-one-year-
old, who'll be forever haunted by what she saw?"
he asked.

Neal said he wanted to "take responsibility for
the whole thing. I will not accept less." On the
other hand, he added, "I want to live and my
only chance is to tell the truth."

There was one last mitigator that he said he'd
forgotten to mention and that was that he no
longer posed a threat to society. He paused, then
shrugged. "I never expected to do what I did,
but I did it."

By the time Neal finished with his opening remarks, it was late afternoon. Judge Woodford de-
clared the court in recess.

September 21, 1999

The next day, the prosecution began its case
by calling Deputy Michael Burgess to the stand.
The balding, mustachioed deputy seemed reluc-
tant to speak about his part in the events of July
8, 1998. Little wonder, nine years on the force
and he'd never seen or even imagined a greater
horror, and it had stayed with him.

Under prosecutor Tingle's questioning, Burgess explained how Holberton's coworkers had

called the sheriff's office, worried because she hadn't come to work for several days, and he'd been dispatched to conduct a welfare check. He talked to a neighbor and failed to get an answer at the front door when he went around back and slid open a glass door.

Calling out, he began to enter and then stopped in his tracks, "overwhelmed by a sense of evil. I saw what appeared to be a body, mummy-shaped, wrapped in plastic," he testified. "I could also see a woman's leg, duct-taped to a chair."

As the deputy spoke, Tingle placed several photographs one at a time on a projector so that they could be seen in the monitors around the courtroom. A photograph of a plastic-encased, mummylike object. A shot through an open back door in which a woman's leg can be seen duct-taped to a chair leg.

"What were you thinking and feeling?" prosecutor Tingle asked. That sort of question would normally have elicited an objection from a defense attorney arguing about its relevance. But Neal was representing himself and would raise no objections throughout the proceedings. He just sat waiting for Burgess's answer while his "advisory counsel," Randy Canney, slumped in his seat.

"It was one of those scenes where you know you just don't want to be there," Burgess said. "A wave of evil hit me. It looked like a torture chamber where somebody had suffered. I knew I needed to get help."

Jose Aceves, the sheriff's lead investigator on the case, was called to the stand next, this time by Bachmeyer. Aceves didn't wear his emotions on his sleeve like Burgess, and it was hard to gauge his expression beneath his thick Fu Manchu mustache as he spoke deliberately and without emotion, recalling his role on July 8, 1998. He'd arrived on the scene and had been told that there appeared to be three bodies inside the West Chenango address.

"Did you check for vital signs?" Bachmeyer asked.

Aceves shook his head. The first officers on the scene had checked for vital signs "and there were none." They'd then retreated from the scene to wait for Aceves and a search warrant.

Once allowed inside, they had recorded the scene with both still photographs and video, which were now shown to the panel of judges as Aceves narrated. There was the filthy, cluttered room, the empty food-and-drink containers. There was the blood splattered on the walls and floor near the chair; on the ceiling above the chair was a trail of blood where Neal had swung his weapon back up to strike again and again.

It only got worse. There was Angela Fite, slumped over in the chair to which her arms and legs had been bound. The position of the chair and the way that the cigarette butts spilled from an ashtray indicated that the suspect had been seated there for some time with a view of his victim in the chair, Aceves said. Fite had been identified by her driver's license, which had been left on her lap and now appeared on the video.

The judges sat grim-faced as the image of a black plastic mummy appeared on the screens. "Rebecca Holberton was found inside," Aceves noted. The audience gasped when a close-up revealed what the investigator said was a piece of skull, bloody strands of hair still attached. "It belonged to Rebecca Holberton."

The video camera zoomed in on a maul that was found in a hall closet. Just a few steps from where the women were murdered, Aceves said. Long strands of human hair belonging to Candace Walters and Angie Fite had been found on the maul, as was the blood of all three victims.

Behind the chair was another body beneath a blanket, the head encased by a white plastic bag. "Candace Walters," according to Aceves.

At last, Aceves stepped down. The photograph of Angela Fite in the chair remained on the screen during a fifteen-minute break. When the court reconvened, Tingle asked that the television cameras be turned off and that no photographs of the next witness be taken or her name published. The media had agreed that such requests would be honored in exchange for the right to have cameras in the courtroom for most of the hearing.

Tingle turned toward the gallery. "Your Honor, the state calls Suzanne Scott."

Seventeen

A petite young woman rose from the first pew behind the prosecution table. A little over five feet tall with blond hair and wire-rimmed glasses over her light blue eyes, she looked timid and helpless as she approached the gate separating the gallery from the rest of the courtroom.

If the case had gone to trial, Suzanne Scott would not have been allowed into the courtroom until after she had testified because she would have been needed to officially identify Neal in court as the man who had raped her and murdered Angela Fite. However, as he had already admitted to the crimes, she was free to attend.

The prosecutors had told her that she didn't need to be present except when it was her turn to testify. She had avoided the preliminary hearings, but felt that she needed to be present for the opening statements. Throughout the first day she had generally stayed within the protective shadow of her mother or boyfriend; occasionally, she sought quiet conversation with a family member of the other victims, all of whom watched over her as though she were a child of their own.

Now she kept her eyes locked on Tingle, who escorted her to the dais in front of the judges. Passing within a few feet of Neal, she kept her eyes averted. She was met by the bailiff, who asked her to raise her right hand and swear to tell the truth before she climbed up into the witness stand. Once seated, she stated her full name for the record as Neal stared up at her profile from the defense table.

"How long have you been in Denver?" Tingle asked.

"My entire life," she answered. Her voice was so soft that she was asked by Judge Woodford to move closer to the microphone, which she did self-consciously by sliding her chair forward.

Tingle was worried. He wasn't going to be able to testify for her. If she resorted to mumbling one-word replies, it was going to be difficult to get across to the judges the horror that she had witnessed. He'd feared that would be the case after he and Bachmeyer had interviewed Scott a month before the hearing. They wanted to brief her about what to expect, but also get a feel for her as a witness. If she had been adamant about not wanting to testify, they would have understood and gone on without her.

Just reading her account of what had happened and hearing Neal's own version, they had been impressed with her strength and courage, as well as her quick thinking. She'd been terrorized with dead bodies, seen a woman brutally murdered, been sexually assaulted with a gun to her head, and yet had the presence of mind to ask Neal to sit next to her on the mattress so she could keep an eye on him. She had done whatever it took to stay alive. No one could have blamed her if she just wanted to forget about it and try to go on with her life. But she understood how vital her testimony would be and never expressed the slightest hestitation about going forward.

They knew that she was scared to death, and Tingle had expressed his doubts to his cocounsel that she would be able to handle testifying in the presence of Neal, but Bachmeyer had disagreed. Maybe it was because she was a woman, but Bachmeyer thought that the same bravery Scott had shown in that house of horrors, she would exhibit in the courtroom.

Tingle started off with easy questions—where she was from, her job—to get Scott focused and comfortable before he gently moved her toward that horrible night. He asked her about late 1997 when she and Beth Weeks were roommates and they were frequenting Shipwreck's, where she first saw and heard about a guy named Cody Neal.

"Do you have any specific recollection about how Mr. Neal was dressed when you would see him?" Tingle asked.

"Yeah, he always had a black cowboy hat on," she replied. "When it was colder, he would wear a longer black, like a duster, coat and always wore boots . . . always in blue jeans. . . . Mostly what I remember is black T-shirts."

"What was your understanding, if you had any, about his financial situation by May and June of 1998?" Tingle asked. He leaned against the side of the lectern facing her, relaxed as if talking to someone at a cocktail party. His voice was soft, guiding, as he kept his eyes on Scott's.

"At certain times, it would seem like he had quite a bit of money, and he was not discreet about having the large amounts of money," she answered.

Good, he thought, *she doesn't need prompting to give complete answers.* "Can you elaborate for us?"

"There was an occasion before my birthday and he comes and gave me a hundred dollars for my birthday," she recalled. "At that time, we weren't that close of friends, I don't believe." She recounted the night that she had been sleeping and her roommate asked if it would be OK for Neal to wish her a happy birthday. "Then Cody came in, and he had a hundred dollars in one-dollar bills. . . . He just threw them all over my bed, and he just, you know, said that we could use that when we went out to celebrate for my birthday."

Scott recalled how she'd met Angela Fite at the bar with Neal. She believed that they were a couple, but Beth Weeks started seeing more of him. "She was really starting to care about Cody more. . . . Their friendship had just really gotten a lot closer."

In mid-June he was talking to her about coming to work for him in what he said was the mortgage-lending business. "When he told you about his business and made this job offer, did you believe him?" Tingle asked.

"Not wholeheartedly," she replied, shaking her head. "With the amount of money that he was talking about . . . and the split of time in the offices between Las Vegas and Colorado . . . it really just seemed mostly too good to be true. And I didn't see why he would be offering me something like this."

Neal told her not to mention his offer to anybody. But when he said he wanted her to go with him to Las Vegas to meet with his lawyers about the job, she broke down and asked Beth if she thought he could be trusted.

"We talked about it for quite a while, and she said that she didn't think that he would ever do anything to hurt us." For the first time in her testimony, Scott faltered. Her voice cracked, and she wiped briefly at her eyes before regaining her composure and pressing on. In the gallery, Beth Weeks began to cry.

Both women remained tearful as Scott recounted how the three of them had gone out on the town after his proposal to marry Beth.

"When that was happening," Tingle asked, "what was the attitude of Mr. Neal? What was his demeanor?"

"He was very happy, calm," she replied. "He was in a really good mood, you know, like he was happy that Friday night was there, and we were going to have such a good time that night."

Tingle nodded. The remarks about Neal's demeanor at this point would be important later, in closing arguments when he would ask the judges to remember the chronology of events. By 7:00 P.M. Friday, July 3, Rebecca Holberton had been dead and wrapped in black plastic for more than three days. He had split Candace Walters's head open only eight hours earlier and left her lying under a blanket. He was in a grand mood indeed.

After dinner at the strip club, Scott said, "he was still in a good mood. Laughing and joking and enjoying himself." Then it was off to the country-western bar, where Wild Bill Cody held court, lecturing the younger bucks how to behave like a proper gentleman.

"That they should stand up when a lady comes

back to sit down," Scott recalled, "and a lady shouldn't light her own cigarettes."

Beth Weeks and one of the young men got into a drunk disagreement until Neal stepped in. "Cody just spoke up and told that guy . . . that he needed to be polite and nice to her."

Tingle paused and looked at the floor for a moment. All the groundwork was now laid. . . . Within days and hours of brutally murdering two women, the polite, respectful man in the orange jail jumpsuit the judges saw in front of them was playing jokes, spending his victims' money on strippers and booze, and lecturing other men on how to treat a lady.

Now came the tough part. Scott had held together remarkably well with Neal looking back and forth from Tingle to her when questions were asked and then answered—like a spectator at a tennis match. Her testimony had taken the morning and started again after the lunch break. It was now time to open the wound. A horrible but necessary step to make sure that Neal never hurt anyone else again.

Softly, without changing his position at the lectern, in a tone that warned her what was coming, he said, "I would like to talk about July the fifth, Sunday." Scott nodded, her eyes closed for a moment, and then she looked up and let out her breath. She was as ready as she would ever be. Under Tingle's guidance, she recounted how Neal had picked her up for their "flight to Las Vegas" and how he'd coaxed her into the garage of the town house on West Chenango Drive by saying he had a surprise for Beth that he wanted to show her. "He explained that it would be more or less like a dress rehearsal . . . that he wanted me to be blindfolded and he wanted to put duct tape on my mouth because that was how Beth was going to do it when she walked into her surprise."

"What was his attitude and demeanor like at that time?"

"He seemed excited and, you know, like this was a great thing that we were going to be working on together."

The atmosphere in the courtroom was tense. Everyone knew what was to come. Tingle looked at the clock and suggested to Judge Woodford that it was a good time to break for the afternoon recess. To himself, he thought it would allow Scott a chance to catch her breath and collect her thoughts.

Fifteen minutes later, Scott was back on the witness stand. "He had me take off my glasses. Then he tied a piece of bath towel around my eyes . . . and then asked me if I could see out of the blindfold."

Neal had her take his arm as he led her through the garage and up the steps into the town house. Inside, he picked up his cat. "He wanted me to meet his cat and he had me pet his cat." He then led her down a hallway; she knew then that something was wrong. For one thing, there was no carpeting in the hallway, just bare plywood, but more than that: "It just didn't feel right," she said.

Still blindfolded and gagged, she was brought into a room where Neal turned her around and told her to sit down. The seat was farther down than she had figured and she quickly realized that she was sitting on a mattress.

In court Scott couldn't remember if he told her that he was going to tie her up or if he just did it. He quickly bound her wrists and ankles with nylon rope to eyebolts screwed into the floor at each corner of the mattress. She was spread-eagled and on her back. Helpless.

Scott hesitated and then began to cry quietly. Tingle waited and soon she pulled herself together enough to press on. "I didn't want to be . . . I didn't want to be tied up," she said, "so I started to cry, and I asked him to just let me go. And I promised that I wouldn't say anything to anybody about what had happened so far. He just told me to shut up, and he said that I hadn't seen him be cold and mean and that I didn't want to.

"Once he tied me up, he opened my blouse and cut off my bra, and he cut off my pants, and he cut off my underwear." She couldn't see the knife that he was using. But she could hear her clothes being cut from her body, and she could feel the cold steel against her skin.

Neal told her to "just be calm and to do what he said and to not cry anymore."

"Do you remember what you were thinking?" Tingle asked.

"Mostly I was thinking about not crying."

"Did you know what was going to happen to you?"

"I had a feeling about what was going to happen."

Tingle picked up a large plastic bag with a pair of pants that had been split along the seams. "Do you recognize this?"

"Those are my pants," Scott acknowledged.

"What do you remember happening . . . after Mr. Neal cut your clothing?"

"He asked me if I had ever seen a human

skull. I said no, and he left the bed and came back with an ice-cream wrapper," Scott said quietly, wiping at the stray tears that rolled down her cheeks. "He pulled out a piece of bone. . . . He held it in front of me, and he was touching it. . . . There was hair on it and he said, 'Can you see that?' And then he laid it on my stomach."

"What was his attitude and demeanor like when he did that?" Tingle asked.

"Just like he was showing off, like 'Look at what I have.' "

Spectators in the gallery began to sniffle as Scott plunged further into her nightmare. Detective Aceves sat hunched over at the end of the prosecution table, looking down at the floor.

One of Chris Bachmeyer's hands came up to cover her mouth and chin. She was still troubled by the nightmare of women being called from a room to their deaths and was having difficulty not crying in court as she imagined the young woman before her in fear, tied up and helpless.

At the defense table, Neal's head swiveled back and forth from prosecutor to witness. Canney slumped in his seat, staring at the table, the law books in front of him closed.

"Were you able to move?"

"No."

"What did he do when he put that piece of human skull on your stomach?"

"I think that he just watched me to see what my reaction would be."

Neal removed the piece of skull and tossed it over onto the black plastic object that Scott could see to her left. He'd been crouching at her side but now stood and walked past a chair at the end of the mattress and over next to the fireplace.

"He lifted up a blanket that was by the fireplace, and he held up a leg," Scott said. "I could see a leg and a sock and a shoe. . . . That's when he said that the black plastic was a body, too. . . . Then he kicked the black plastic bag. . . . He kicked it hard."

"What was going through your mind at this time?"

"I just thought I was going to die because I didn't understand why he would show me what he did and then let me live," Scott said matter-of-factly. Her courage on the stand had spectators shaking their heads in admiration, but there was more . . . and it only got worse.

Scott recalled how Neal warned her of "the others" upstairs and then left her covered with a blanket, thinking of the horror surrounding her, not daring to move. When he returned, she could hear him whispering with another person, who was seated and bound to the chair that she'd seen at the foot of the bed. "He asked, 'So how's your day going so far?' " She recognized the voice of the woman who answered as belonging to Angela Fite.

When he lifted the blanket, "I think it really took Angie by surprise. She just looked at me, and she shook her head, and she said, 'I'm sorry.' . . . Then she said, 'We're not going to get out of here alive, are we?' "

Neal seemed to be in no hurry. After allowing Fite to have a cigarette, he retaped Scott's mouth.

"Tight enough to hurt?" Tingle asked.

"It was uncomfortable, yes," she replied. "And

so then he said he was going to get a treat for his cat." He disappeared from her sight for a moment before reappearing behind Angela with the maul half-raised. "Then I saw him hit Angie," Scott recalled, sobbing. Her family, Angela Fite's family, Candace Walters's daughter, Rebecca Holberton's sister, Beth, and other friends cried as well.

Then, as if he'd finished some chore, Neal calmly walked away. When he returned, he stooped to pick up the cigarette that had popped out of Angie's mouth.

Scott recalled how she could hear Angela's blood striking the wood floor . . . not one drop at a time but "like water pouring from a pan." Neal got up and placed a blanket under Angie's head—"so you don't have to hear that."

Fite had been saying things that she wasn't supposed to, he explained. That's why he'd done what he had to do. "You see how calm and smooth I am," he boasted. "Bet you didn't know that was coming."

Scott told the judges how she had been forced to kneel next to Angela Fite's body and perform oral sex. In his seat at the defense table, Neal shook his head as though in disbelief.

"He was holding the gun to my head, and I asked him if I was going to die," Scott said, crying. "He asked if I wanted to die. I said no."

"How was he holding the gun to your head?" Tingle asked.

Scott lifted her left hand and pointed it like a gun to her temple. "Like right here," she said.

"Could you see that gun?"

"No."

"Could you feel it?"

"Yes, I could feel it."

Scott cried quietly and Tingle allowed her a minute before asking her to describe the rest of the rape and then the long night of terror. Spectators shook their heads at the courage that she'd shown by asking him to sit on the mattress and hold her hand. "I just wanted to have him next to me so that I knew that he couldn't sneak up on me," Scott explained. "He sat with me all the rest of the time that we were there."

"All night long?" Tingle asked, though he knew the answer.

"Yes."

"Did you hold his hand?"

"Yes."

"Why did you do that, Suzanne?"

Her answer poured from her like water through a shattered dam. "So that if I fell asleep, that I would feel him move his hand so that I could wake up, and I would see what he was doing so he couldn't sneak up on me like he snuck up on Angie."

The rest of the afternoon passed as Scott recounted each event in detail. "Do you have words that you could use to describe your mental state during this, Suzanne?" Tingle asked.

She hesitated, then said, "I kept expecting . . . I kept thinking that Angela was going to move. I kept thinking that person that I saw, they were going to move. I just kept thinking that somehow this wasn't true." The image of Angela Fite's feet and hands still taped to the chair stuck in her mind. "I still see that a lot. . . . I think I memorized exactly how it looked when I left."

Scott wasn't sure how long she and Beth Weeks were forced to sit and listen to Neal recount his rampage into the tape recorder. When at last she was allowed to go to her bedroom, she shut the door and turned on the television, hoping to go to sleep. That next morning, she said, she tried to stay in bed as long as possible "so I wouldn't have to go out into the living room."

When Neal warned them not to try to get help and left them alone, she said, they both "just kind of wandered around our apartment aimlessly."

"What was going through your mind about those threats?" Tingle asked.

"Just that he meant it," she replied. "I didn't think that he would hesitate at all to hurt me or to hurt Beth. It just seemed like whatever we could think of to do to get help, wouldn't work . . . wouldn't work good enough or fast enough."

Scott recalled how David Cain came into the picture—choosing to stay with the women rather than ensuring his own safety. When Neal left and the police arrived, "Beth and I were basically hysterical . . . and I don't know that we were making sense to anybody. Dave was still on the phone, and so it was very chaotic when they first got there."

Scott's testimony was nearly over. She'd done better than Tingle could have ever imagined from someone who had been through so much at such a young age, at any age. She'd recounted as horrible a story as any he'd encountered in fifteen years as a prosecutor, sitting just a few feet from the man whose face haunted her waking hours as well as her sleep. It had not taken much prodding; neither was Scott weepy, afraid to speak. Yes, she *had* cried, but at the right moments, when anything less wouldn't have seemed natural.

It was time to let her go and hope that someday she could put it behind her. Never forgotten, but less immediate. There was just one more image he wanted to leave the judges with. He asked her about the afternoon after the murder of Angela Fite when Neal insisted that they drive back to West Chenango Drive.

"We had gone by it and he said we may have to go back inside just this once," she recalled. "I just begged him again and asked if he would please not make me go back into that house."

"Can you tell us what was going through your mind?"

"It was scary," she replied. "There wasn't anybody there. The police weren't there at that time and I was very afraid that I was going to have to go back inside, and I didn't want to see what was inside again. . . . I was afraid if I went back inside that I wouldn't come back out."

As Scott spoke, Tingle shuffled through his photographs. Finding the one that he sought, he placed it on the overhead projector so that it would appear on the television monitors around the courtroom. The image of a beautiful, smiling young woman appeared.

"Who is that?" Tingle asked.

A cloud passed over Scott's face. "That's Angie," she answered softly.

Tingle told the court that he had no more questions. Scott began to move as though to get down from the witness stand, but froze when Judge Woodford asked Neal if he wanted to cross-examine her. Up to this point, she had not looked at Neal, but if he questioned her, she would have to; she didn't turn to see his response.

"Your Honor, I do not," Neal said.

With that, Scott was excused. She stepped down from the stand, her head up and eyes on her mother as she moved past Neal.

The court was adjourned for the day. The spectators, many of them still in tears and sniffling, filed out quietly. The family and friends of the victims were gathered at the elevators to leave when someone noticed that Beth Weeks wasn't with them. There was a moment of panic. . . . There was no evil that they would put beyond Neal's capabilities. But she was in the hallway, sobbing as a victim's advocate placed an arm around her shoulders.

"It was my fault," Beth moaned. "It was all my fault."

Eighteen

The next day, Beth Weeks got her chance to testify against her onetime lover, the romantic, exciting, mysterious millionaire who was going to buy a home for her and her children. He had seemed like "the same old Cody," she recalled, when he picked her and Suzanne Scott up on the evening of July 3, just a few hours after hacking Candace Walters to death.

He proposed to her, she said, a joke. Of that she was sure. He'd then lived up to his reputation, spending money freely by taking his dates to a strip bar for dinner and a dance. Then later, holding court at The Stampede, instructing the young men how to treat a lady.

A few days later, when he sat in her kitchen and explained what he had done to the three murder victims and her roommate, "it was like he was proud," she said, breaking into tears and sobs. "I screamed at him. . . . He put a gun to my head and asked if I wanted to die."

Then he'd made her sit there with him as he taped his confession, a nightmare that "went on and on and on until the sun came up," she recalled. "He said he had killed Angie because she had lied to him and was going back to her husband."

When he gave her, Suzanne Scott, and David Cain instructions on what to do after he left them, he warned that he was a hit man for the mob and would kill them all if they deviated from his plan. She'd believed him.

Most of the rest of the day was occupied with testimony from criminalists who described the meaning of various pieces of evidence, such as the blood-spatter analysis.

The fourth day of the hearing was devoted to the videotaped interview that Neal gave Aceves and investigator Cheryl Zimmerman on September 14, 1998. When told it would last eight hours, Judge Woodford asked if an excerpted version could be played instead, but Bachmeyer insisted that the panel hear the full tape. The prosecution team didn't want any defense attorneys coming along later and claiming that an excerpted tape made Neal look worse than he was and using it as the basis for an appeal.

A former National Park Service ranger and seven-year veteran of the district attorney's office, the forty-one-year-old Bachmeyer had spent the past couple of years before this case working domestic violence cases. It bothered her that given the outlandish stories that Neal had fed to his victims, they would come across to the public as witless and gullible . . . as having gone almost willingly to the slaughter like sheep.

She knew the victims were not stupid. They were all intelligent, caring women. They did not engage in lifestyles that put them at risk: they didn't hang out with gangs; they weren't prostitutes or drug addicts; they didn't go out with strangers. Neal was no stranger to these women; he was their friend, confidant, and lover.

But they were vulnerable in one way or another to a sweet-talking con man—maybe they were in a bad relationship or just getting out of one . . . or struggling to make ends meet . . . or simply lonely. Then along came Wild Bill Cody, in his cowboy hat and boots, with his wild, exciting stories, tossing money around like a millionaire. But more important, tossing around all the answers to their dreams, all the right words that they wanted to hear.

He was so detailed in his lies—that was what was mind-boggling to her. He even had a photo album with pictures of his "mansion" in Las Vegas and the mansion down the street from his that he'd supposedly bought for Candace Walters. He would play on the heartstrings of women . . . crying, in a manly sort of way, over his beloved mother's death and vowing to fight to win his little girl back from her "evil stripper" mother. He chose victims the same way that a farmer selects fruit off a tree—picking the ripe ones, the ones ready to fall.

Bachmeyer hadn't had as much personal contact with Neal as Tingle—she was handling other aspects of the case, such as talking to his ex-wives and family members—but what she did have was more than enough. He immediately struck her as someone with an almost desperate need to be liked, whether it was by the guards, the police investigators, or even the prosecutors who were trying to kill him. But she felt his demeanor toward her went beyond friendliness to flirting, testing to see how Bachmeyer, an attractive blonde, would respond.

"Hi, Miss Bachmeyer," he'd say when he saw her, smiling and twisting his head to make eye contact if she didn't look him right in the eye. "Don't you look nice today," he'd add, no matter how conservatively she dressed. If he heard she'd been on vacation or had a few days off, he'd want to know how it went.

Maybe it was just paranoia, knowing how he operated on women. She wasn't his type anyway—she was happily married, and too self-confident, too successful, too aware of what he was doing. To her, he came off as the sleazy guy at the bar, the one with all the pickup lines.

Neal would be the one who knew them all.

Bachmeyer thought that the full version of the video would give the judges a more complete picture of Neal: his animation as he imitated how he'd raised the ax to dispatch his victims; his ability to control conversation; his constant attempts to manipulate the investigators with compliments, threats, and promises to divulge everything in exchange for things he wanted. She wanted the judges to understand how dangerous Neal really was—that the murdered women had been taken in by a real sociopath. "Better than Ted Bundy" was how he'd described himself.

The victims weren't stupid, nor were they greedy. Sure they wanted their money back, but the extravagant amounts that he promised them only surfaced in the last few days as the lies that he'd been juggling began to fall. A look behind her at the packed courtroom was proof that they were good mothers, good friends, and very much loved.

Neal had been the picture of decorum in the courtroom. Polite. Pitiful. Contrite. Bachmeyer

hoped that the tape would help the judges see
him for what he really was . . . a ruthless predator. She pushed the play button.

On monitors around the courtroom, Neal suddenly appeared as he had looked a year earlier.
Still in the orange jumpsuit, he had long hair
and a dark goatee. The questions and answers
jumped from the monitors like the script from a
horror movie.

> *Q: Was it like an adrenaline rush?*
> *A: No . . . The adrenaline rush would come*
> *when I would kill somebody, like being a High-*
> *lander.*
>
> *This was different to me, all right? Because I*
> *cared about them.*
> *Q: You like to take charge of the situation?*
> *A: I'm a strong-willed person. . . . I mean, if*
> *somebody has to make a decision, let it be me,*
> *because right or wrong, I'm going to make it. I*
> *mean, somebody has got to be a leader.*
>
> *I need prosecution. I need justice to be served*
> *because I'm representing three dead people . . . as*
> *well as a rape victim. I want justice to be served*
> *and the truth to be known so that people can get*
> *on with their lives.*
>
> *I mean, you know, if I had told her I'm going*
> *to take you to the house, and I'm going to tie you*
> *down, and I'm going to rape you, and you're go-*
> *ing to witness a murder, she's not going to go. . . .*
> *I'm not being sarcastic with you at all, Jose.*
>
> *I was good at covering things or putting so*
> *much shit out, pardon the French, that everybody*
> *that thought they knew me ain't even stinking*
> *close. They don't even know the first color of my*
> *hair.*

You get in trouble and you go to God. Well, that's sometimes the only time that He's able to get through your thick skull, all right?

My mother killed me, OK, period. . . . If my mother was alive right now, she would be there for me in a heartbeat. Now, she would not pat me on the back. She wouldn't dance and kick her heels. She would not say, "You did the right thing, killing those people." . . . It would have probably killed her. But she would have still stood with me.

Rebecca was the most gentle, loving, sweetest person you ever knew. . . . I was never mean to Rebecca, never hurt Rebecca, never beat on her.

I'm great at business, whether you want to believe it or not—marketing, sales, you know, bullshit, con. . . . People are greedy, so I use that.

If somebody is angry, they don't care. They just hate you so much or want to get a piece of your ass, right, they're going to walk blind. That's why you shouldn't ever make a decision in anger, right, because chances are you're making the wrong one. You've got to be cool; you've got to be calm; you've got to be thoughtful.

Q: Do you hate women?
A: Not that I am aware of. I mean, it's not in my conscious mind. A psychiatrist might say deep down I hate women.

This is a warning: Don't fuck with me, all right? Don't open your fat mouth, OK? You better keep yourself quiet or you're going to die, all right?

I felt bitter in a way, but . . . I didn't use bitterness with that ax in my hand splitting her brain to execute her, right?

I'm not here just for a piece of ass. I'm here for somebody to love me and love somebody else, one on one.

I raped a woman. . . . If Suzanne was the only crime I ever did in my life, I would hope you would execute me for it. That's how I feel about rape, OK?

It's not like I had a woody raising the ax up and killing them, all right? I executed them. I wanted them to go as quickly as possible. It was not a sexual turn-on for me to kill somebody. I was not thinking of sex in any way when I murdered Rebecca, Angie, or Candace. It had nothing to do with saying, "Look, bitch, for all you other ones cheating on me in the past. . . ."

Q: *Why did you choose a maul?*

A: *It had weight to it; I knew it would be enough to kill. . . . I believe, even though I haven't yet experienced lethal injection, it was a lot more compassionate and fair to kill them like that. Even though it didn't look real pretty, it was instant, OK? Meaning,* boom, *dead. And if they weren't dead and just throbbing, so to speak, they sure as hell weren't thinking about the pain.*

Damn right I pitchforked that cat, all right? . . . I went in there and was going to pet the cat because I like animals, I always have. I pet them. I went over to pet him, and this cat just tore into me. And my temper when I was young . . . I grabbed this fork, and I just pitchforked this thing. . . . I mean, it's like they put animals to sleep for biting somebody. I mean, what's the difference? It attacked me; I defended myself; I killed it—simple as that.

I had a dog that bit me one time, and I killed him, too. And then I had a puppy that bit me that I killed. It was mean. It was just like something was wrong with him. I punched his brain in . . . just, boom.*"*

*You got to remember one thing: even a good
liar makes mistakes and forgets things.*

*I was trying to spare Rebecca the nightmare
that her financial world might be coming to a
close. . . . She was greedy; she wanted to retire
from the phone company. . . . She was going to
be buried. She was going to be a slave. And, you
know, I grieve over that.*

Q: *Why did you urinate on Candace Walters?*
A: *It was, like I said, the ultimate humiliation. . . . It was like, you know, "Lady, you're
gone. My life is gone. Rebecca. Angie. Careful
where you dig." . . . It was like an Oriental martial arts thing or an Indian thing. I mean, I
hope somebody pisses on me when I'm gone, all
right?*

*If I can murder something I love, what am I
going to do to some bastard that I don't love or
have any respect for? I'm going to tear him up.
Then you're going to know what torture is.*

*I don't believe Ted Bundy deserved to die . . .
or even me. But justice is justice. The difference
between them and me was that I was judge, jury,
and executioner all in one, OK? . . . But I gave
fair warning.*

*I'm more agitated right now than I was
then. . . . It was like a normal, relaxed state. I
wasn't angry to where I said like, "Fucking bitch,
boom!"*

*I didn't want to put a gun to their heads or a
shotgun to the back of their heads and blow their
heads off, I mean, because of the neighbors, you
know. And then I [would have] had to kill the
next-door neighbor and the painter and . . . It's
like if the neighbor would have come over, I'd have
killed the next-door neighbor. I would have just*

gone ahead and went on a real killing spree. I mean, you guys would have had to pump a bunch of lead in me, all right?

Q: What about your claims that you were a bounty hunter and a hit man?

A: It was all just an act, playing a part. Bundy put it in a good way, not that he was an idol, but there was certain things that he did that were close to me. He said that the more you practice it, you were like an actor, an illusion, that you sold somebody that you were somebody that you weren't. That the more he practiced lying or acting the role, the better he got and the more natural he became. . . . I related with Bundy in a lot of ways. Not because he was a mentor with me, I was better than Bundy would have ever been, OK? I'm not meaning that bragging, but I've had this killer in me all my life, and I've depressed it.

I don't believe that I believe my own bullshit. That's why I had an argument with mental health. They kept saying, "Do you hear voices?" No. Nobody told me to do it. I'm just a stinking liar, OK?

Like it says in Revelation, Revelation 6:8, about this pale horse, and on it was a rider, and his name was Death, and Hades followed him. That's me, OK?

When at last the tape ended, the courtroom was silent. Stunned, numbed. *"That's me, OK?"* The judges looked as drained as everyone else in the courtroom. Bachmeyer hoped that the tape got across the contrast between the man who could discuss extremely graphic violence without flinching in September 1998 and the contrite, "I've found Jesus" defendant who delivered his own opening statements saying that he was a changed man.

Neal was a walking contradiction of everything he claimed to be. He said that he loved animals, yet he pitchforked a cat and punched in the skull of a puppy. He claimed to have been raped and haunted by the trauma of it, yet he raped the most innocent young woman that he could find. He said he loved Rebecca, Candace, and Angie, yet he robbed them, duped them into thinking he had arranged for something to make their lives better, then split their skulls open with an ax.

Neal was right about one thing, Bachmeyer thought, he was a predator. If not "better than Bundy," then straight out of the same mold.

The next prosecution witness was Dr. Ben Galloway, the forensic pathologist, who drew a red circle on the back of a Styrofoam head that he was handed by Chris Bachmeyer. He was nationally recognized as one of the best in his field—a veteran of more than nine thousand autopsies, many of them the victims of violent crime. He'd never seen worse than this.

In a courtroom, he came across as friendly and warm, a country doctor, even when matter-of-factly describing where the two-and-a-half-inch piece of skull had flown from Rebecca Holberton's head. The wound, he said, was consistent with her having been struck there with the blunt end of the maul.

There were also defense wounds on Holberton's hands, Galloway testified, indicating that for all of Neal's supposed care to kill instantly, she had reacted to that first blow by raising her hands to her crushed skull. However, the destruction was massive as the back half of her brain had been "mashed" and fragments of bone had pierced deep into her brain. But she'd been dead and decomposing for more than a week before her autopsy, and it had been impossible for him to determine how long she may have lived after the attack.

Candace Walters was another story. She'd been struck hard with the sharp edge of the maul twice above her left ear, above her right ear, and again at the base of her neck, along with other more superficial cuts, according to Galloway.

"How long did it take for her to die?" Bachmeyer asked.

"Three to four minutes," the doctor answered. He knew that because there had been blood in her airways from aspiration and swelling in her lungs that wouldn't have occurred after death.

Angela Fite had also lived for several minutes after being struck six times on the head, neck, and back, Galloway testified.

As the autopsy photograph of Angela was produced on the monitor, there was a gasp from the gallery. "Oh, my God," a woman sobbed. "Oh, dear God."

"Were you able to determine the cause of death?" Bachmeyer said. It seemed like the answer was clear, but it was still a necessary legal formality.

"Each died from massive trauma to the head," Galloway answered.

Charles Tingle wrapped up the prosecution case by calling the victims' family members to the stand. He'd asked them to write letters to the deceased describing the impact of their murders on them. He told them that he was going to ask them to read them aloud in court, knowing that otherwise it would be difficult for them to speak without breaking down. There was one caveat: they could ask for justice to be served, but the law prohibited them from asking for a specific punishment.

Of Holberton's family, only Debbie Lacomb, her sister, made it to the trial; her mother had Alzheimer's disease and hadn't been told of the murders. There wasn't much that she could say about Neal, she'd never met him, but when it was time for her letter, Lacomb cleared her throat and read aloud:

"Dear Rebecca, I want to tell you how much I love you. I'm sorry I never really told you that before.

"I miss you so much. I even miss the arguments we used to get into sometimes. I miss talking to you about Mom and the funny things she does. She asks about you quite often, wondering where you are, but I don't tell her.

"I have your ring. I wear it all the time. It makes me feel close to you, like you are with me.

"It makes me so sad to think of how awful your life must have been those last few months. So full of pain and sorrow. I wish you would have told me what was going on. Maybe, in some way, I could have helped.

"You will always be with me. I will see you again in another place, a happier place free of pain and sadness."

Holly Walters was next to take the stand. She wore her blond hair short and looked coldly at

Neal through her wire-rimmed glasses. She'd taken it upon herself to be the main spokesperson for the families to the press. The strong one . . . but it was just a brave face now that the best part of her life had been taken from her.

She'd been unable to even get through her letter the night before without breaking down entirely. The hardest part of the trial for her had been listening to Neal on the tape describing how "cute and studious" her mother had looked sitting on the chair as he approached with his ax. Until he bashed her head in, she thought, wondering how he could have gone from one to the next as though choosing what to have for dinner. Most people that she knew didn't equate "cute and studious" with wanting to murder somebody.

Ever since her mother's death, she had lived for the day when she could confront Neal and verbalize what he had taken from her. She wanted to look in his eyes and try to understand the person behind them. Seeing him from the witness stand, she found it difficult to comprehend that he'd looked at her mother with those same baleful blue eyes as he prepared to kill her.

Like many other family members and friends of the victims, Holly wanted more than anything to get one point across: Neal picked intelligent, attractive women for his targets, and he was a master at finding out where they were vulnerable. The women all had dreams and hopes . . . and he'd offered them a glimpse of a better future with his money and attention.

With one last look at Neal, Holly Walters turned her attention to Tingle, who asked her how long she had lived in Colorado. Twenty-six years. The prosecutor produced a photograph of her mother. "Who is that?" he asked.

Holly smiled. "That's my mom, on Mother's Day, 1997. I'd popped over to let her know I had not forgotten."

Under Tingle's gentle questions, she recalled growing up the only child of a single mother. "I was fortunate to have a mom who spent a lot of time with me. . . . We were extremely close. The older I got, the closer we got." They had enjoyed going on almost-daily walks in the hills near where she lived.

"Her dreams were simple . . . a house and a dog and as much free time as possible to enjoy her hikes."

Neal, she said, was charismatic and caring . . . sitting with her mother all night after work just talking in a booth. He invited her to a New Year's Eve party. "He was renting a whole floor at the hotel."

The relationship got "fairly intense, fairly quickly," which was unusual for her mother, who had last been in a committed relationship several years before her death, but had said "she was going to stay away from men." Holly paused, then added while looking at Neal, "I wish she had."

Holly Walters was concerned about the man with all the tall tales and seemingly endless supply of money. But her mother was "happier than I had ever seen her" and so she'd let her misgivings slide. She wasn't supposed to know about the promises that Neal was making. "He was very explicit about that," she said. Concerned about her mother's loans to Neal and his mysterious ways, she was the one who suggested that they try to find out more about him.

The last time Holly Walters saw Neal, they had both just arrived at her mother's apartment. "He gave me an extremely warm hug. He was in a very, very good mood. He could be quite charming when he wanted," she said, turning to face the defendant, who looked quickly away.

Holly told the court about the trip that her mother had planned with Neal, the outlandish promises of money. Then the foreboding and the trip back from Missouri, knowing as each mile passed that something was wrong. She talked about reaching Neal on his cell phone and his lie about the accident with the deer.

When he was through asking her questions, Tingle asked Holly Walters to read her letter. She looked down at the piece of paper and took a deep breath. She knew she had to get through it somehow:

"Dear Mom, there is so much I want to say to you, so many things I want to share. And I am hoping that this letter finds its way to you somehow. I have been struggling to find a reason for all that has happened, and why it was you that had to be taken from me. Of all the people in this world, I will never understand why someone who loved life so very much and had so much to offer, had to be the one to fall.

"My life has been changed forever and words can never convey how very much I miss you. I miss your laughter, your smile, your warmth. I miss the comfort your hugs once brought me. I miss the walks, the conversations, the silence we shared on Sunday afternoons, when all we needed was each other's company. I miss sharing my life with you.

"In the silence of my quiet moments, I try and remember each detail of our lives together and the details of you as the person that you were. I listen for the sound of your laughter in my mind, the tone of your voice; I imagine your bright blue eyes and your tender touch . . . although it often brings me to tears, the memories are bittersweet.

"When I walk, I try and take familiar paths that we once walked together, remembering the conversations, the happiness I felt at that time. I feel the breeze and wonder if you are there with me still, if you can feel me trying to hold on to you.

"I want you to know that I haven't forgotten all that we experienced together . . . or all that you taught me. From the simple things like roller-skating and cooking to the important things like how to treat others, to live my life as full and as passionately as possible, and to take advantage of each moment I have here on this earth. I am still learning from you, and I ask myself each day if I am doing things like you would have wanted, to take my time with people and try and send love out to those less fortunate.

"Although I can hardly imagine bringing a child into this world at this point, I know that one day I will. I regret that my child will not have a grandmother to love, and God knows I could use your guidance. But I will do my best to teach my child who you were, and what you were about. The beliefs and morals my child will learn are yours, and so a piece of you will be passed on, and my love for you will be shared. I love you, Mom. You were . . . You ARE the best Mom I could have ever been blessed with. I hope I can make you proud, and that you are up in Heaven right now, smiling down on me."

It was not in her letter, but Holly had one more thought as she came to the end and looked again at Neal. "I never thought that someone who meant so very little to me could take so much from me."

Angela Fite's sister, Tara, climbed up into the witness box and turned cold eyes on the defendant. She'd gone ahead with her July 25 wedding to Jeb; for those weeks leading up to the event, though, she often woke in the morning and didn't want to get out of bed. But her mother insisted that Angela would have wanted her to go on with her life.

When she thought of her sister and what she'd been through with the last two men in her life—Matt Rankin and Cody Neal—she could only believe that Angie was happier now. But she missed her and was grateful that Jeb had a way of calming her in the worst moments.

She was haunted by nightmares. The night before her wedding, her three bridesmaids and stepbrother from her father's second marriage were spending the night at her house when the subject of Neal came up. "What if he has friends?" one of the bridesmaids said, voicing a fear that they all shared. The women decided to spend the night sleeping in the same bed. They even persuaded Tara's stepbrother to sleep in front of the bedroom door.

That night Tara had another nightmare. In it she was awake and listening in the dark to the sound of someone crawling on the ground around her bed. Then she realized that the noises were being made by a skeleton as it crept nearer to her. She could not scream but only make a strangled "mmmmm" sound.

Realizing that Tara was having a bad dream, one of the bridesmaids touched her to wake her. Tara grabbed her arm and bit her, hard, and the young woman screamed, which startled the others out of their sleep, as Tara's stepbrother burst into the room. Someone managed to turn on the lights, which helped calm the situation, but they got up and went to the living room where they remained awake all night.

Tara would experience more nightmares, including one in which she woke up screaming during her honeymoon. But there was also one other dream, one that helped her get through the next year.

Again she dreamed that she was lying in bed, on her stomach with the covers down, listening to the sound of something crawling toward her. Only this time, the sound was replaced with the feeling of someone blowing gently on her back. Turning over, she found herself looking into the face of Angie. Her sister looked beautiful; her blue eyes were clear and bright, her cheeks and lips pink. Angela was smiling and it was then that Tara knew it was all right to go on with her life.

Tara had thrown herself into her studies to become an emergency medical technician (EMT). Sometimes Angie's death didn't seem real. She'd drive by Angie's old apartment and nearly stop, thinking, *I should go see if she's home*. Then she'd remember and it would hurt all over again. For a year, she'd seen a counselor to help her cope with anxiety attacks.

All because of Cody, she thought as she approached the witness stand and considered bolting for the defense table to try to kill him. But she knew she'd never get there or accomplish the task. All she could do was continue forward and be sworn in before taking the stand. She looked at Neal and was overwhelmed by a feeling of disgust. If only he knew how sick just looking at him made her feel.

Tara described how her sister's murder took away her "zest for life" just three weeks before her marriage. "Angie was always smiling. She was always happy," she recalled for the judges. "All she wanted was a nice, healthy home for herself and her children. And someone to care for her, love her, and treat her with respect."

She testified that she'd met Cody once "and was not impressed. I thought he was full of bullshit." But her sister believed his lies "because she wanted all that so bad."

At one point, she said, Angie had mentioned that she thought Neal was going to ask her to marry him. But toward the end, she was ready to get away from him. "She said, 'I'm about there,' " Tara said.

Frequently, as Tara testified, she turned to face Neal, her eyes blazing with hatred. He couldn't hold her gaze. But he wiped at his eyes, as did many in the gallery, when she recounted how when Matt Rankin told Angie's son Kyle, five, who was responsible for killing his mother, the little boy cried, "No, Cody was my friend. He bought me a bear."

Matt Rankin would take the stand to testify how Angie was the "only woman I ever really loved." The prosecution did not dwell on how many times he'd been arrested for hurting her.

Lastly, Betty Von Tersch walked slowly to the witness stand. After Angie's death, Betty had lived under a cloud so long that she wondered if she would ever see the sun again. She cried every day and talked to her murdered daughter, asking for her help. Like Tara, she sometimes forgot that Angie was gone . . . would think about calling her or going by to visit. . . . Then reality would return and so would the tears.

Valium kept the nightmares at bay for the first couple of weeks. When they came, most she could not remember, other than they left her disturbed and depressed. However, there was one that she recalled in which she entered a house filled with men wearing black shirts and black ties. "Mafia hit men" were the words that came to her sleeping mind. All the men were dead, having killed each other; their bodies, the walls, the floors were covered with blood. Angie was in the basement, hiding, as Betty Von Tersch had hoped to hear in those days following the arrest of Neal. *"You'll never believe what happened, but I'm OK."*

Sometimes she wished she could be with her eldest daughter. But there were two reasons to push on: Kyle and Kayla. They'd been told about their mother's death, though spared the details.

It was for the two of them, and her love for her surviving daughter, that Betty Von Tersch found the strength to keep going. Now she just wanted the three black-robed judges to know her daughter. Angie, she began, was a straight-A student and "a good little girl."

Angie had told her that she thought Cody might have been a hit man for the mob, but that it was in the past and even then he had "only gone after bad guys." When she asked her daughter when she could meet this mysterious man, Angela had replied that he wasn't ready to meet her family yet.

On Saturday, July 4, Angela was happy; the next day, Cody was going to show her "the surprise he had for her." It was the last time that they ever saw each other.

"Everybody handles it a little differently," Betty Von Tersch told the judges. "Everybody hurts a little differently. I've cried almost every day for a year and two months." Kyle cried, too, she added. Kayla, too young to grasp what happened, toddled around the house, hugging pictures of her mother, picking up a toy telephone to call her mother "in Heaven" to say, "I love you, Mommy."

Betty had also prepared a letter for her deceased daughter.

"To My Dearest Little Angel Angie," she read aloud, "I miss you so much. I wish I could physically just see you and talk like we used to, hold you and let you know that everything will be OK, even if only for one minute.

"When I learned of your death, a darkness prevailed over me for many months and at times reoccurs. When Cody took your life, he also took a huge part of me that can never be replaced. At that point, my life changed forever.

"Every day I try to accept the fact that you are gone and you are not coming back. Someday, after time, I think that peace will come to me. I cannot accept the tragedy that happened to you.

No one deserves to die the way you, Candace, and Rebecca did. Not one of you girls wanted to die. You did not have the chance to make that choice.

"I do know in my heart that even though we have had those beautiful memories of our happy times dimmed by life's hardships and struggles and the darkness and gloom of a gruesome tragedy, that the love and bond between a mother and daughter never dies.

"The loss of a child is the most painful experience a mother will ever endure. . . . There are a lot of missing pieces to this whole thing that I still do not understand and may never, until I see you again. Please give me, and everyone in our family, the strength to understand this so we can someday have a normal life again.

"For the rest of my life and even beyond, I will do everything I can to love, protect, and care for your babies, Kyle and Kayla. I love them as much as my own children. It breaks my heart to know your children will grow up without their mother. They have been deprived of the love, hugs, kisses, and comfort of their mom. Your family is giving them that for you with all we have to give.

"Sweetheart, you never deserved what happened to you. You were a person who had a heart of gold and cared about people. Unfortunately, this awful thing did happen and now we all have to deal with what lies ahead. . . . I love you, sweetheart. My heart and soul are with you every minute of each day. I miss you so much."

As Betty Von Tersch read, tears streamed down the faces of the families in the gallery as they tried to stifle small cries. Neal again wiped at his own eyes. In his opening statement, he had asked for "reconciliation and forgiveness." His answer then, and as Betty climbed down from the witness stand, was a resounding no.

"Your Honors," Tingle announced, "the state rests."

Nineteen

William Lee "Cody" Neal's defense was short, just a handful of witnesses. Like a real lawyer, he called each witness to the stand, and asked each to "state your full name and spell your last name."

The first was Byron Plumley, Neal's spiritual adviser since August, when he called the professor at the university and expressed remorse for his actions. Plumley began his testimony with a caveat, "I can only say what I've seen and heard." However, he added, Neal had "what you call 'surrendered' to God and the judgment of this court."

When Neal asked him to describe his defense strategy, Plumley replied, "Your defense is rooted in what you believe that God is asking you to do," and that included not cross-examining the government's witnesses or objecting to prosecution evidence or testimony.

"All men have the spark of the divine in them," Plumley concluded, saying to Neal, "I believe that you have the spark of the divine in you as well." But, he added, "only time will tell if your transformation is a permanent one."

The rest of Neal's witnesses were investigators and guards, who were called to testify regarding his behavior since his capture. One of those was Jose Aceves. Neal asked him if having met him, the investigator would have believed that Neal "fit the description" of the man who committed the murders.

"No," Aceves acknowledged, looking as though he'd rather have his teeth pulled than be up on the witness stand, fielding questions from Neal.

"Do you believe that I've killed other people?" Neal asked.

"Based on information from you?" the investigator replied. "No . . . but we don't know for sure."

It wasn't long before Neal had called his last witness. It was late Friday afternoon, and he asked the court for the weekend to think over whether he would testify. Judge Woodford granted him the time.

On Monday the court reconvened and Neal announced that he'd decided not to testify. If he did, the prosecution would have had the right to cross-examine him. However, he said he wanted to make a statement of allocution, which would not be given under oath or on the witness stand and therefore not open to cross-examination.

Standing at the defense table, Neal essentially repeated his opening statement. He noted that he lived up to his promise not to cross-examine the victims' family members or other prosecution witnesses. He acknowledged that his crimes deserved no mercy, but said that he wanted to live so that he can "serve God in prison."

He asked, "How could anyone have mercy on someone like me? To those three beautiful women that I ruthlessly murdered, I gave no mercy, or they would be here today. So I find it difficult to ask that of this court. The man that did that deserves none."

But, he added quickly, he was not that man anymore. "My heart was stone, and only God can change a heart." With that, he thanked the court and sat back down.

Charles Tingle rose from his seat and walked to the lectern to deliver his closing arguments. In the final analysis, Tingle believed that Neal's demand to represent himself was based on several issues: one, that he was "throwing himself on the mercy of the court"; two, that if he received the death penalty, he could convince an appellate court to rule that he wasn't competent to represent himself; three, and maybe the most indicative of Neal's character, he was a control freak. In control of the women. In control of their money, their emotions, their lives. He tied his rape victim to a bed to control her. And now he wanted control over the proceedings to determine if he lived or died.

"Mr. Neal stated in his opening that when he committed the brutal, heinous murders of Rebecca Holberton and Candace Walters and Angela Fite, that on some level it was like casting a stone into a pond, that the ripple effect touched the lives of everyone.

"In retrospect, that stone was more like a bombshell and those ripples more like tidal waves. People have not been merely touched by the heinous murders that Mr. Neal committed.

People's lives have been shattered; their futures have been destroyed.

"It is not merely enough to say that they have been touched, or that there is pain, or that there is suffering."

Tingle looked at Neal, who was leaning forward in his seat, listening carefully, and glancing up at the judges to gauge their reactions. Tingle shook his head. "I stand before you this morning with an impossible task," he said. "That is, to adequately summarize how the defendant's vicious slaughter of innocent women has impacted the family, has impacted this community, and to describe the magnitude of the loss of life for Rebecca Holberton and Candace Walters and Angela Fite.

"All too often in this business, this sometimes horrible business that we are in, we begin to distance ourselves from what has truly happened from the real human impact. . . . We sit here in the courtroom, a sterile environment, removed by many months, yet we try, through the evidence, to recall what happened, and we try to understand the impact of those crimes. . . . I have struggled and struggled to try to find words that adequately somehow relate what has happened in this case, and I can't."

Instead, he asked the judges to recall the words of the victims' family members:

Dear Rebecca, I want to tell you how much I love you. I'm sorry I never really told you. We love you and miss you. We will never forget you. . . . Mom, there is so much I want to say to you, so many things I want to share. I am hoping that this letter finds its way to you somehow. There is

*no bond so sacred as a mother and daughter
share. . . . My dearest little angel Angie, I miss
you so much. I wish I could physically just see
you and talk like we used to, hold you and let
you know everything will be OK, even if only for
one minute. When Cody took your life, he also
took a huge part of me that can never be replaced.*

What, Tingle asked, did Neal's own words and
actions say about his character? That's one of the
aspects, he noted, that the judges must base their
final ruling on:

"He talked so calmly months later" during his
interview with Aceves and Zimmerman "about
how with each swing, Rebecca's head got 'sloppier and sloppier.' "

On July 1, Neal gave Holly Walters a big hug,
he pointed out. "He was in a great mood as Rebecca Holberton lay dead in the living room of
her town house."

On July 3, with Candace Walters dead only a
few hours, Neal was in such a good mood that
he playfully asked Beth to marry him. "That
someone can play a practical joke, hours after
committing two savage murders . . . Does that
say something about his character?

"Mind you, the defendant is good. He is good.
Able to convince Rebecca Holberton, Candace
Walters, Angela Fite, Suzanne, of unbelievable
things."

Pointing at Neal, who blinked several times
and swallowed hard, Tingle said, "He knew Kyle
and knew Kayla, and he murdered their mother."
The prosecutor placed the photograph of Angela
Fite, still taped in the chair, back on the overhead. "What does it say about the character of

a man who forced Suzanne into oral sex just inches from the body of a dying woman?" he asked.

The prosecutor played excerpts from Neal's confession. "I was better than Bundy would have ever been. . . . I had a killer in me all my life. . . . A pale horse and the rider is Death with Hades following. That's me."

Tingle cautioned the judges not to believe Neal's assertions that he had "turned back," as he liked to quote a Turkish philosopher. "Those words have no meaning coming from him. He is a manipulator of the highest degree, a schemer, a con artist of unequaled ability.

"He does not deserve your mercy. Your compassion should be reserved for his murder victims. . . . The death penalty is justice. To be merciful and not impose the death penalty is wrong, for to be merciful to the cruel is to be indifferent to the good."

Tingle took his seat. Judge Woodford asked Neal if he wished to make a closing argument. The defendant leaned over to Canney and said something to his advisory counsel, who shrugged. Neal shook his head. "I said what I wanted to say in allocution."

And that was it. That was "the strategy" that Neal would not reveal to anyone. That was the end result of all those telephone calls, all that time in the law library, the stacks of death penalty materials that he'd demanded.

Woodford announced that judges would render their decision in two days, on Wednesday, September 29. The court was adjourned.

* * *

During their deliberations, the three judges found that the state had proved all of its aggravators, with only minor deviations. They then rejected all of Neal's mitigators. More than that, they spurned everything that Neal had to say for himself.

They didn't believe his claim to have been sexually assaulted in his youth. "Given William Neal's pattern of habitual lying, the panel questions the accuracy of these events," they wrote in the court order that would be handed down with the final sentence.

They doubted his remorse. "William Neal is so self-absorbed that his capacity for remorse is questionable."

Nor were they impressed that Neal chose not to cross-examine family members in order to save them further anguish. "The panel discounts such concessions, given the overwhelming evidence, prearrest statements, and self-serving postarrest confessions."

Even his religious conversion was "suspect, given the timing."

They threw his words right back at him. "William Neal referred repeatedly to his religious conversion and cited the Bible during his allocution, requesting mercy and forgiveness. The panel also recalls that William Neal used the Bible in his statement to police: 'It's Revelation 6:8, about this pale horse, and on it was a rider, and his name was Death, and Hades followed him. That's me, OK.'

"William Neal claims to be a changed man and, therefore, requests mercy. William Neal cannot point to the past as a basis for mercy but asks the panel to trust him in his promise toward the future. This panel is unwilling to do so. The panel relies upon the past as the best predictor of the future. William Neal's plea rings hollow in light of his past deceits and evil deeds.

"All three murder victims in this case were warm, loving, caring individuals. Each, in their own way, was in a vulnerable position at the time they met and began to interact with William Neal. It is clear William Neal chose them in large measure precisely because of their vulnerabilities.

"All three murder victims came from close-knit families. They shared close bonds. The impact of this murderous slaughter on the families has been enormous. Their grief is immeasurable, and their loss incalculable. An integral part of each family member has been taken from them and can never be replaced. All have suffered tremendously. Beyond all of this is the fact that one day Angela Fite's two children will learn the brutal way in which their mother died and, at that time, will have to deal with this horror yet again."

For perhaps the first time in his adult life, Neal's words had failed to move their intended audience. He was revealed, in his own words, as "just a stinkin' liar."

On September 29, 1999, the Jefferson County courtroom was packed as it had been on the opening day of the hearing. After he and the two other judges took their seats at the dais, Judge Woodford said he would not be reading the thirty-six-page findings of the panel. The panel was there only to announce their verdict.

Cody Neal's eyes were fixed straight ahead on

the panel, his hands clasped in front of him. As
Judge Frank Martinez and Judge William Meyer
stared down at the defendant, Thomas Woodford
wasted no more time announcing that "the only
penalty for the brutal, needless killing visited
upon these kind and lovely ladies is death."

Neal didn't react, other than to blink repeatedly. A single, collective shout—"Yes!"—ema-
nated from the family section of the gallery.
Although he acknowledged that the verdict was
an "emotional issue," Woodford admonished the
crowd to be quiet.

Then, a sudden fright: the lights went out and
the courtroom plunged into complete black as
spectators gasped. The lights came back on even
as the deputies moved to surround their prisoner. William Lee "Cody" Neal would not be escaping his fate on their watch.

Neal was handcuffed and, without glancing
back again, was led quickly out of the courtroom
through a side door. The families and friends of
his victims stood and left, pursued down the hallways by television cameras and reporters all seeking their reactions.

A few minutes later, Randy Canney stood in
the hallway fielding questions from more reporters. On principle he did not believe in the death
penalty, and it had been troubling to have to sit
silently in the courtroom while Neal hanged himself, figuratively if not yet literally. He told the
reporters that he believed that Neal was mentally
ill, delusional, and shouldn't have been representing himself.

Even though Neal didn't want a lawyer, Canney had continued to try to act as one throughout the process, only to be ignored. As a defense

lawyer, he wasn't immune from the horrors per-
petrated by his client. He had to look at the
photographs; his thoughts and dreams were
sometimes haunted by those images. Sitting
through the Neal case without much else to do,
he'd been a witness to all the pain on the faces
of the victims' families and had been moved by
their testimony about how deeply they'd been
hurt. He was used to seeing the varied emotions
of victims or their families. Some were horribly
angry. Some were horribly sad.

A defense lawyer had to compartmentalize
those things so that he could do his job. He had
always wanted to be a criminal-defense lawyer; he
liked the idea of fighting for the underdog
against the state. His first obligation was to make
the prosecution prove its case, but he felt the job
went further than that. It was up to him to paint
his client as a human being, not a monster. It
had been deeply troubling that he had not been
allowed to do that.

Prosecutor Tingle applauded the judges' decision and their rejection of Neal's excuses and
pleas. "This is not a court of mercy," he said.
"This is a court of law."

A half hour after the court was adjourned, the
victims' families met with the media in a room
on the first floor of the courthouse. They had
issued a joint press release that included a complaint aimed at those in attendance who were
morally opposed to the death penalty, such as
Jim Aber.

"We are offended by those who presume to
manipulate the word of God to justify a request
for mercy when such godless acts were clearly
committed in complete absence of mercy."

Sitting at a table, holding up photographs of their lost loved ones for the cameras, they thanked Charles Tingle and Chris Bachmeyer and the investigators "for their commitment and sensitivity."

"This brings some closure, but it does not bring back my mom, Angela, or Rebecca," Holly Walters said.

"This is not going to be over for us for a very, very long time," added Wayne Fite, Angela's father.

They said that they all planned to attend Neal's execution. "To the end," said Wayne. "To the end," Holly repeated.

Epilogue

September 26, 2001

"In retrospect, that stone was more like a bombshell and those ripples more like tidal waves. People have not been merely touched by the heinous murders that Mr. Neal committed. People's lives have been shattered; their futures have been destroyed."

—Charles Tingle

As Chief Deputy District Attorney Charles Tingle knew it would, the ripple effect of William Lee "Wild Bill Cody" Neal's bombshell has continued to wash over the lives of those whom he came into contact with. He has a way of making even his victims' survivors feel guilty; some of them will have to live with that heartache, as well as their loss.

In the months before Angela's murder, Wayne Fite had pushed his daughter away because she would not get out of an abusive relationship with Matt Rankin. What she found was worse, though only by degrees. Rankin, who had testified that he had never loved anyone as much as Angie, will also have to look at himself and ask why

Angie had to look for love and safety in the arms of another man.

In 2000 Angela's sister, Tara, gained custody of Kyle and Kayla after Rankin was accused of neglect and of domestic abuse of his girlfriend at the time. They are both a joy and a reminder of her loss.

All of their lives will never be the same. . . . There is no "getting over it" for the families of murder victims. Betty Von Tersch insists that Tara call her every day "or I'm over there knocking on her door."

"It never stops hurting," she says. Once she went to the hospital complaining of chest pains, but the physicians could find nothing wrong. She didn't know how to tell them that the pains were symptoms of a broken heart.

The families weren't the only ones affected. Deputy District Attorney Chris Bachmeyer, who for some time afterward was haunted by dreams of women dying, recalled being left emotionally "flat" by the trial. "There was no joy. Maybe a sense of satisfaction that the families got justice, but I can't say I was happy. That's not the right word."

Her colleague, Tingle, said, "I hope it gave the families some closure. But it's not over for them. This will drag on for years. As for myself, my biggest emotion was that I was glad it was over. It seemed like for that year, I was walking around day and night with a big dark cloud hanging over my head. I hope it goes away."

The prosecutors and investigators still wonder if there are other bodies buried in Neal's past.

Randy Canney remains troubled that the judges weren't "painted a fuller picture of Cody's life." Had he been allowed to take a more active role, he would have brought in "people who have good things to say about him. . . . It's not like for the past three or four years he's been an absolute con. He can be a nice guy. He was a good businessman. He's a very engaging man.

"Why, when he was forty-two years old, did he suddenly do this horrible thing? While he may not have been the most law-abiding citizen, he had no criminal record. In looking for answers, you have to hope that there's some good in everybody, an explanation for the bad. I don't believe in abject evil. I think there's a reason."

Canney said he didn't know if that "fuller picture" would have changed the judges' minds, "but they should have heard it."

In the meantime, Neal was appointed two appellate lawyers from the Colorado Public Defender's Office. He vacillated between keeping them and firing them—that much had not changed about his personality.

In December 1999, one of Neal's appellate lawyers, Jeff Pagliuca, filed a complaint with the Colorado Supreme Court's attorney-regulation committee, accusing Jefferson County Chief Deputy District Attorney Mark Pautler of unethical conduct that included dishonesty, fraud, deceit, and misrepresentation. The complaint stated that Neal told sheriff's investigator Cheryl Zimmerman that he wanted a lawyer to represent him or he would "not surrender without one." The court's attorney-regulation committee found reasonable cause to go ahead with a formal complaint, and a trial date before a panel of disciplinary judges was set with a potential consequence of disbarment.

Neal's advisory counsel, Randy Canney, noted
that the alledged misconduct could be used by
Neal's appellate lawyers to overturn the sentence.
"It is certainly going to be grounds that the post-
conviction lawyers are going to try to utilize," he
said. However, he told this writer that given the
circumstances, he couldn't fault Pautler. "I would
have probably done the same thing."

Pautler told the media that he didn't believe
that the complaint, even if the court ruled
against him personally, could be used to overturn
Neal's conviction. "It didn't have to do with any
evidentiary matters," he said.

William Tuthill, an assistant county attorney appointed to represent Pautler, defended his client.
"Mr. Pautler spoke to Neal as a 'public defender'
to assist in persuading Neal to surrender," he said.
"The law enforcement objective was to prevent
further bloodshed, and to apprehend Neal without further threat to the public, the officers, or to
Neal."

In January 2001, a judge with the disciplinary
committee ruled that Pautler had committed
misconduct by engaging in "intentional deception," a violation of the ethical rules for attorneys. A hearing was set for March before three
judges with the Colorado Supreme Court's disciplinary judicial panel to determine what, if any,
action would be taken against Pautler.

At the hearing, deputy attorney-regulation
counsel Nancy Cohen argued that Pautler's deception strained already frayed working relationships between the Jefferson County District
Attorney's and Public Defender's Offices.

(This argument made little sense: If Neal had
been upset with the ruse, he should have turned

even more to his defense lawers. In actuality, of
the myriad of issues that Neal talked about in his
letters and conversations with Tingle and Bachmeyer, none had anything to do with Pautler mis-
representing himself as a public defender, or this
being the cause of the rift between him and the
public defenders' office. In fact, Neal repeatedly
told just about anybody who would listen that he
fired the public defenders because he wanted to
plead guilty and they wanted to prevent him
from doing so.)

Cohen argued that a public defender would
have been obligated to advise Neal to turn himself in. Public defender Jim Aber, whom Neal had
fired, and Pagliuca both testified that they would
have faced sanctions if they had not given that
advice. Pagliuca said that Pautler's deception was
to gain a "tactical advantage."

"The notion that if the crime is bad enough,
government lawyers are entitled to lie is a flawed
one," he said, urging the panel to suspend Pautler's license. "Any attempt to justify this kind of
conduct is the epitome of arrogance."

Along with the contention that Pautler was a
law enforcement officer acting within the bound-
aries of that position, Tuthill argued that the
Colorado Rules of Professional Conduct, the por-
tion of the canons that apply to attorney ethics,
states that while lawyers are not supposed to engage in deception, the rules also recognize that
they should be "guided by personal conscience."
Those rules should "exhaust the moral and ethical considerations that should inform a lawyer,
for no worthwhile human activity can be completely defined by legal rules," and were intended to "provide a framework for the ethical

practice of law." Any discipline of the offending lawyer, according to the canons, should take into account the "facts and circumstances as they existed at the time of the conduct in question and in recognition of the fact that a lawyer often has to act upon uncertain or incomplete evidence of the situation."

Jefferson County District Attorney Dave Thomas and other Denver metro-area district attorneys testified on behalf of Pautler saying that they agreed with his actions. Pautler was himself unrepentant. "I'm quite comfortable with what I did that night," he told the panel. "What I did that night I did to save lives and take a killer off the streets."

After the hearing, and while the judges were deliberating, various people weighed in on the charges in the press.

Defense lawyers chastised him, some merely to say that he should have allowed a police officer to effect the ruse. Others contended that his actions put their profession into "even more disrepute." One Missouri lawyer even wrote to a Denver newspaper columnist echoing Pagliuca's "epitome of arrogance" quote. He added, "To permit an attorney to evade responsibility and accountability for violating the very trust they swore to uphold is nothing more than reinforcing a Godlike mentality and belief that they somehow are above the law."

Meanwhile, the court of public opinion favored Pautler. Letters to the editor from police officers and citizens criticized the attempt to censure Pautler.

Russell L. Cook, the police chief of Golden, a city located in Jefferson County, said that Pautler

had put public safety first. "You can appreciate
what Mark Pautler was going through. He had
just been to the scene of the murders. . . . The
images in his mind were of the hideous brutality
Cody Neal had unleashed. He quite possibly
averted a massive manhunt that may have driven
Neal to flee, harm other victims, or take hostages.

"I understand these rules of professional conduct that attorneys operate under. But they are
simply a framework for the ethical practice of
law. You can't have a rule for every single issue
that comes up. It seems to me they could say,
'Yes, this was an exception.' "

Writing for the chapter of the Fraternal Order
of Police, with the Lakewood Police Department,
Detective Patrick Wilson wrote: "It is our understanding that Mark Pautler's actions in July 1998
were instrumental in the apprehension of the
person who murdered three women and who indicated the desire and ability to kill even more
people. Thanks to Pautler's quick thinking, there
were no further deaths and the killer, William
"Cody" Neal, has been sentenced to die for his
heinous deeds.

"Now because of his heroic actions, Pautler is
being prosecuted by a group of lawyers who obviously have little contact with the realities of the
criminal-justice system and even less understanding of dealings with killers.

"Many of us have worked with Pautler on murder and other cases during the past sixteen years,
and we know he only does what is right and what
best protects society.

"As Lakewood police agents, our job is to en-
force the laws justly and fairly. We are outraged
that an agency such as the Attorney Regulation

Counsel would prosecute one of the finest and fairest prosecutors we have ever worked with, or anyone else, for doing what was necessary to prevent further killings and to bring to justice a triple murderer."

Betty Von Tersch wrote as well. "As the mother of Angela Fite, who was brutally murdered by William "Cody" Neal in July 1998, I am shocked and very disturbed to learn that the Attorney Regulation Counsel is prosecuting the person who caused Neal to be arrested as quickly as possible without further deaths or harm to our community. . . . It is hard to believe that Pautler could be found guilty of misconduct for his actions, which brought my daughter's killer to justice.

"I believe that Mark Pautler is a hero for what he did. Not only should he not be sanctioned . . . he should be praised for having the courage to do what he did to stop William Neal's killing spree."

Neal's surviving witness, Suzanne Scott, added her own letter. The only reason that she had been able to go on with her life, she wrote, was because of the "heroic" actions of Pautler.

In the end, the judges handed Pautler one year's probation. Still, too much for his supporters.

Meanwhile, as of February 2002, the courts were still trying to determine when to hold a new competency hearing for Neal. His other appeals couldn't begin until that matter was cleared up once and for all.

Neal was offered the opportunity to comment for the purposes of this book. In September 2000, he contacted this writer for the first time since the

July 28, 1999, interview with him at the Jefferson County Detention Center. He requested that the writer provide him with numerous documents and newspaper articles, including a two-part series of stories the writer published in *Westword*, a Denver weekly, in October 1999, in exchange for his renewed communication.

Only the *Westword* article was sent. His response was to "rebuke" the articles and the writer as having been the instruments of Satan, who, he said, had "typeset" the piece, and to refuse to cooperate in the writing of this book. He enclosed his diatribe in an envelope on which he'd printed a number of biblical warnings, among them: "He who guards his lips guards his life, but he who speaks rashly will come to ruin." Proverbs 13:3. . . . "A false witness will not go unpunished and he who pours out lies will not go free." Proverbs 19:5. . . . "Hatred stirs up dissension but love covers over all wrong." Proverbs 10:12. He signed off with: In His Service, Cody Neal.

Manipulating, always manipulating, that's Wild Bill Cody. He was very good at it. Maybe not better than Bundy, but out of the same mold. One of the most difficult aspects for the families of Neal's victims to deal with has been that the women were somehow at fault. How could they have believed his stories? What made them so gullible?

But many women have fallen for Neal's lies and deceits, his charms, and his ability to make himself whatever they wanted or needed, to reach out and touch their dreams and make them believe that he was the guy who could make them come true.

Holly Walters knows she will spend the rest of her life wishing she had looked harder into Neal's life. But her mother was usually very selective about the men she got involved with—and she was so happy.

"My mother was an extremely trusting person who gave a lot of herself in relationships and expected a lot in return," Holly said shortly after the hearing. "I think she was tired of being alone, and he offered her the moon. He had a charisma she found irresistible.

"But it was never about the money. . . . The really outrageous numbers he was throwing out only happened in that last week. For none of these women was it about the money. It was everything to do with his presence and the way he communicated."

Like many other family members and friends of the victims, Holly is adamant about getting one point across: Neal picked intelligent, attractive women for his targets, and he was a master at finding out where they were vulnerable.

"These women had dreams and hopes," she said. "He offered them a glimpse of a future."

There are four other women who can attest to the damage that Neal has done: his former wives. Although they survived their marriages to him, they still bear scars.

Jennifer Tate attended only the opening statements of his death penalty hearing. She saw the ring that he was wearing and thought for a moment that it might have been the wedding ring that she'd given him. When she realized it wasn't, she felt sorry for whomever he had won over with his lies for a fifth time.

Even his opening statement was an act. For

one thing, he claimed to have never read anything more demanding than a dictionary as part
of his "aw shucks, good ol' boy" routine for the
judges. The man she knew could quote Thoreau
and Voltaire.

It made her ill to hear how he'd sucked in
Candace Walters with that story about wanting
custody of their daughter. Of the two years between their daughter's birth and their divorce, if
she totaled every day, every hour, and every minute that Neal spent any time at all with their
child, it would have amounted to "maybe two
months," she said.

"All the photographs I have of him and her,
he has this expression of 'Hurry up and get it
over with.' Only when he was in public and trying to impress people did he ever act like she
was his."

Tate has met a young man closer to her own
age, not particularly well schooled in romance
but absolutely dedicated to family life. Together
they are raising her first child plus his from a
previous marriage, and a baby that's theirs. They
live in a little house, where Tate is content to be
a stay-at-home mom. She couldn't be happier . . .
except for the fear that Cody Neal will find a way
to get at her from prison. The fear is so great
that even after he was placed on death row, she
hardly let their daughter out of her sight.

When Karen Wilson learned of the murders,
she didn't know where to turn. The district attorney's investigators in Colorado were kind as
they listened to her story, but she knew that it
had to be hard for them to understand how a
woman could fall for Neal's lies and manipulations. She wished that there were someone she

could talk to who would understand. Then one of Neal's sisters put her in contact with Tate, who was dealing with the same waves of guilt and fear, and somehow they found courage together.

As they got to know each other, Wilson recognized that Neal had treated Tate, and probably every other woman he'd ever met, the same way. That's why, despite her fear, it became so important to her to let the families of his victims know that this behavior wasn't new. He didn't suddenly snap. He'd been building toward this—if, indeed, this was his first act of murder, and she had her doubts about that—for a long time.

"The thing that made these women so wonderful, trusting, loving, were the things that made them targets," she said. "He found things in all of us that he could exploit. I just hope someday to be able to convey to the families that it could have been any woman in their daughter's and mother's shoes. None of us were stupid.

"He's just the con artist from hell. There was nothing they could have done to stop him from picking those women. If he wanted them, he was going to get them."

Some days she wonders if he ever loved her. Whether the creature hiding behind that smile and those blue eyes was even capable of love. "All I know is that life, and love, is not about bubble baths and rose petals," she said. "Be careful, and if you ever run into a man named William Lee Neal, turn and walk away."

ACKNOWLEDGMENTS

The author would like to thank those who assisted in the writing and publication of this book. He wishes to express his admiration to those victimized by William Lee Neal who had the courage and strength to help tell this story so that Rebecca Holberton, Candace Walters, and Angela Fite are not forgotten, nor the memory of them sullied by the many lies and manipulations of their killer—thanks particularly to Betty Von Tersch, Tara Brewer, Holly Walters, Karen Wilson, and Jennifer Tate. We would do well to remember, too, that Angela Fite was a victim of violence before she met Neal; domestic violence remains a largely hidden but deadly serious epidemic in the United States. The author also expresses his gratitude to the Jefferson County District Attorney's Office—David Thomas, Mark Pautler, Pam Russell, Charles Tingle, and Chris Bachmeyer, as well as Defense Attorney Randy Canney—for their candor in so far as the code of professional conduct would allow them while Neal awaits the results of his appeals process. As always I am grateful to my agent, Michael Hamilburg, and his consigliere, Joanie Kern, for their faith and hard work, and to my gem of an editor at Kensington, Karen Haas. To my family, my love and thanks for being the antidote to the poisons of monsters like Wild Bill Cody. For anyone who might wish to create some good from this tragedy, please contribute to: The Memorial Fund for the Benefit of the Children of Angela Fite, Wells Fargo Bank, Southwest Plaza, 8500 W. Bowles Avenue, Littleton, CO 80123.

MORE MUST-READ TRUE CRIME FROM PINNACLE

illusions
white Camd. Petals

MORE MUST-READ TRUE CRIME
FROM PINNACLE

Slow Death   0-7860-1199-8 $6.50US/$8.99CAN
By James Fielder

Fatal Journey   0-7860-1578-0 $6.50US/$8.99CAN
By Jack Gieck

Partners in Evil   0-7860-1521-7 $6.50US/$8.99CAN
By Steve Jackson

Dead and Buried   0-7860-1517-9 $6.50US/$8.99CAN
By Corey Mitchell

Perfect Poison   0-7860-1550-0 $6.50US/$8.99CAN
By M. William Phelps

Family Blood   0-7860-1551-9 $6.50US/$8.99CAN
By Lyn Riddle

Available Wherever Books Are Sold!

Visit our website at **www.kensingtonbooks.com**.